Modern Economic Sciences on Environment, Growth and Information

Modern Economic Sciences on Environment, Growth and Information

Edited by
　Koshiro Ota
　Aya Nushimoto
　Keiji Tagami
　Hiroshima Shudo University

Volume 16 in a Series of Monographs of Contemporary Social Systems Solutions
Produced by the Faculty of Economic Sciences, Hiroshima Shudo University

Kyushu University Press

Volume 16 in a Series of Monographs of Contemporary Social Systems Solutions
Produced by Hiroshima Shudo University

All rights reserved. No part of this publication may be reproduced or transmitted in any form or by any means, electronic or mechanical, including photocopying and recording, or by any information storage and retrieval system, without the written permission from the publisher.

Copyright © 2025 by Koshiro Ota, Aya Nushimoto and Keiji Tagami

Kyushu University Press
744 Motooka, Nishi-ku, Fukuoka-shi, 819-0385, Japan

ISBN978-4-7985-0383-7

Printed in Japan

Preface

This book, titled *Modern Economic Sciences on Environment, Growth and Information,* is the 16th volume in the Series of the Monographs of Contemporary Social Systems Solutions since 2005. The Faculty of Economic Sciences at Hiroshima Shudo University, which is the producer of the Series, makes it the educational and research objective "to conduct systematic education and research on actual economic phenomena and problems, and furthermore on various phenomena and problems related to management, society, and the environment, by significantly introducing various modern sciences, including information science." In the society in which we live, new economic phenomena and problems are emerging one after another, which can be the subject of our education and research, and the scientific means to analyze them, especially in the field of information, are constantly evolving. This series is positioned as a medium for publishing the results of ambitious and meaningful research that meets these educational and research objectives. The title of this book also strongly reflects their themes. The book consists of the following six chapters.

In Chapter 1, Masayuki Hiromoto reveals how policy networks are formed and function. Specifically, the author clarifies the policy networks of officials dealing with farmland at Yokohama City Government in Japan. Yokohama City is the municipality that possesses the biggest population in Japan. In 2020, Japan had eleven cities that exceeded one million in population. Among these big cities, Yokohama City enjoys high outturn of agriculture. Yokohama City Government assists agriculture by preserving farmland against urbanization. The author addresses a question of why Yokohama City Government is willing to maintain farmland. The finding is that career paths of directors at the department of agriculture are characteristic in Yokohama City Government and induce preservation of farmland. Many directors of the agricultural department in Yokohama City Government experienced posts concerned with environment before assuming the chiefs of the agricultural department. Directors of the agricultural department form policy networks with people involved in not only agriculture but also environment. Therefore, the directors tend to regard farmland as a protector of environment as well as a place of economic activity.

In Chapter 2, Hiroki Iwata analyzes the technology choices of firms in oligopolistic markets using a two-stage game model. First, firms choose between production technologies that involve negative externalities and green technologies, followed by either quantity or price competition. In addition, this study addresses a situation where the negative externalities generated by firms affect their production costs. This is a situation in which not only negative externalities arising from the firm's own actions, but also negative externalities generated by other firms affect production costs. The analysis demonstrates that, when such effects are present, firms can have incentives to voluntarily adopt technology that reduces their environmental burden under Cournot competition. In contrast, under Bertrand competition, voluntary adoption of technology to reduce their environmental burden does not occur. Additionally, the introduction of an environmental tax under these circumstances has the effect of promoting the adoption of environmentally friendly technology in the Cournot market, but its effect would be limited in the Bertrand market.

In Chapter 3, Shohei Katayama develops an endogenous growth model and investigates the dynamics and growth of the Japanese economy. The Japanese economy has encountered secular stagnation for thirty years. The growth rate, inflation rate, and the interest rate have been low. And the population is decreasing. The performance of the Japanese economy greatly changed in the 1990s. Hansen argued the secular stagnation in the 1930s. Summers, Gordon, Acemoglu and Aghion etc. revived the secular stagnation after the world financial crisis. The secular stagnation was argued from demand side and supply side. Japan has encountered the secular stagnation for thirty years and thus the author mainly considers it from supply side. The author develops a model of endogenous growth, in which growth is generated by a random sequence of quality-improving innovations. It is called Schumpeterian because it embodies the force that Scumpeter called "creative destruction." In the context of a Scumpeterian model with capital accumulation, the capital stock and the innovation rate are jointly determined and influence each other. Therefore it can bring the rich and effective growth policies for Japan. The author also mentions the effects of decrease in population on the economy.

In Chapter 4, Hiroyuki Dekihara, Toru Ochi, Minori Kurahasi, and Masafumi Imai build a new image classifier that evaluates and classifies the proficiency and skill of device users. With the development of information technology, many people use information devices such as computers, tablets, and smartphones. These devices are used in various situations, such as education, business, and daily life. It is indispensable for developers of novel devices and researchers in ICT education and other related fields to collect, analyze, and feedback extensive and effective data on the actual and major patterns of input methods among PC users in order to supply new services and make further improvements. In this research, the author develops a means of measuring input methods: Keyboard and Flick Inputs. The means of measuring has adopted MediaPipe by AI Library to record and analyze these movements in both the keyboard and the flick input method with an inexpensive web camera. Then, the author builds a novel image classifier by LightGBM which is a gradient-boosting framework that uses tree-based learning algorithms and is able to classify users into several groups based on the user's levels: typing speeds, typing styles, etc. The classified results enable us to evaluate the proficiency and skill of users, recognize the situation of progress like class, work, etc. and give feedback to them. The image classifier and the development method will be expected to contribute to evaluating and recognizing the actions of PC users, workers, learners, etc.

In Chapter 5, Keiji Tagami discovers a new relation between a knot invariant, which is called "flat plumbing basket number" in his study, and 3-dimensional contact geometry. Mathematically, a knot (or link) is an embedding of some circles into a 3-space. Knots have been studied in the field of geometric topology for a long time. Recently, many specialists in knot and link theory have been interested in relations between knots and 2-, 3-, and 4-dimensional geometry. In particular, there have been many studies on knots and links in contact 3-manifolds. In this study, the author gives a new approach to the study of knots and links in contact 3-manifolds. In particular, the author considers a surface consisting of a disk and some untwisted and unknotted bands, and embeds it into the trivial open book decomposition of the 3-sphere. Such a surface is called a flat plumbing basket. It is known that such a decomposition of a 3-manifold induces a contact structure on the 3-manifold by Thurston-Winkelnkemper construction. By utilizing this property, the author relates the number of bands of the surface with contact invariants of the link appearing in the boundary of the surface. This relation induces an inequality, which is one of the main results of this manuscript, between "flat plumbing basket number" and contact invariants of links, where the "flat plumbing basket number" of a link is defined by the minimum number of bands among flat plumbing baskets whose boundaries are the link. As an application, the author proves that for torus links, the three values: flat plumbing basket number, maximal self-linking number and maximal v-degree of HOMFLYPT polynomial are essentially the same.

In Chapter 6, Setsuko Sakai and Tetsuyuki Takahama address the improvement of methods for solving multimodal optimization problems. Multimodal optimization is a very difficult task to search for all optimal solutions at once in optimization problems with multiple optimal solutions. Speciation using proximity graphs has been studied as a method for solving multimodal optimization problems. It has been shown that speciation-based particle swarm optimization with β-relaxed relative neighborhood graph (SPSO-G/βRNG) can search for many optimal solutions with high accuracy. In multimodal optimization, search points are divided into some species and each species searches a different region, so it is necessary to enhance the local search ability. In this study, the authors propose three methods to improve SPSO-G/βRNG by enhancing the local search ability: introducing sphere mutation, introducing local mutation, and adjusting PSO parameters. In sphere mutation, in order to search the immediate vicinity of a candidate of optimal solutions, a random search is performed within the hypersphere whose center is the candidate and whose radius is the distance to the nearest search point. In local mutation, a mutation operation in differential evolution (DE) is used, where the difference vector is selected from neighbor search points rather than from all search points. In the PSO parameter adjustment, a large value of cognitive parameter and a small value of social parameter are adopted. The performance of the proposed method is shown by optimizing well-known benchmark problems for "CEC'2013 special session and competition on niching methods for multimodal function optimization."

Finally, the editors would like to thank Mr. Shunji Nagayama, Editor of Kyushu University Press, for his great contribution to the publication of this book. We would also like to thank Professor Jun-ichi Maeda, Dean of the Faculty of Economic Sciences at Hiroshima Shudo University, for his great encouragement. This book was supported by the budget of the Faculty of Economic Sciences at Hiroshima Shudo University in fiscal year 2024.

November, 2024
Koshiro Ota
Aya Nushimoto
Keiji Tagami

Contents

Preface i

Chapter 1 The Yokohama City Government's Organizations and Personnel in the Fields of Farmland and Agriculture .... *Masayuki Hiromoto* 1
   1. Introduction 1
   2. Methodology 6
   3. Results 11
   4. Discussion 16
   5. Conclusion 17

Chapter 2 Negative Externality and Green Technology Adoption in Oligopolistic Markets .... *Hiroki Iwata* 21
   1. Introduction 22
   2. The Model 23
   3. The Effect of Environmental Policy 29
   4. Discussion 32
   5. Concluding Remarks 33

Chapter 3 Dynamics and Growth Policies of Japanese Economy .... *Shohei Katayama* 35
   1. Introduction 35
   2. Facts of Japanese Economy 36
   3. Representative Models 41
   4. Policies for Growth 48
   5. Conclusion 50

Chapter 4 A Development of the Image Classifier to Classify Computer Users Based on Tracing Data of Keyboard Typing
.... *Hiroyuki Dekihara, Toru Ochi, Minori Kurahasi and Masafumi Imai* 53
   1. Introduction 53
   2. Proposed Method 54
   3. Experiment 56
   4. Conclusion and Future Plans 61

Chapter 5 Flat Plumbing Basket, Self-linking Number and Thurston-Bennequin Number
Keiji Tagami 63

1. Introduction 63
2. Preliminary 65
3. Legendrian Link from Flat Plumping Basket 67
4. Maximal Self-linking Number and Flat Plumbing Basket 70
5. Maximal Thurston-Bennequin Number and Flat Plumbing Basket 73
6. Further Discussion 75

Chapter 6 Improving Speciation-Based Particle Swarm Optimization with Graphs by Sphere Mutation, Local Mutation, and Parameter Adjustment for Multimodal Optimization
Setsuko Sakai and Tetsuyuki Takahama 81

1. Introduction 82
2. Proximity Graphs 83
3. Speciation 85
4. Multimodal Optimization Using SPSO-G/βRNG 86
5. Proposed Method 90
6. Numerical Experiments 92
7. Conclusions 95

Contributors 101

Chapter 1

The Yokohama City Government's Organizations and Personnel in the Fields of Farmland and Agriculture

Masayuki Hiromoto
Faculty of Global and Community Studies, Hiroshima Shudo University
1-1-1, Ozuka-higashi, Asaminami-ku, Hiroshima 731-3195, JAPAN

Abstract

This study clarifies the features of the Yokohama City Government's bureau in charge of farmland and agriculture in Japan. Yokohama City has the highest population among the municipalities in Japan. In 2020, Japan had 11 cities with more than one million people. Among these large cities, Yokohama City enjoys a high outturn in agriculture. The Yokohama City Government assists agriculture by preserving farmland against urbanization. This study addresses why the Yokohama City Government can maintain farmland. The bureau, which existed from Fiscal Year (FS) 2005 to FS 2023, and its high-ranking officials responsible for farmland and agriculture in the Yokohama City Government, held characteristics that induced the preservation of farmland. The bureau contained the departments of the environment and parks, as well as the departments of green zones, including farmland, and agriculture, and regarded farmland as a place for environmental protection and relaxation. Many high-ranking officials in charge of green zones and agriculture held positions concerned with the environment or parks before they achieved the designation of director general or executive director. The bureau and high-ranking officials responsible for farmland and agriculture could regard farmland as a place for environmental protection and citizens' relaxation, rather than for declining economic activities.

Keywords: Large city, city government organization, farmland, agriculture

1. Introduction

Nerima Ward Government in Tōkyō Metropolis, Japan, held an event to sell vegetables cultivated in 24 urban municipalities such as Kyōto City, Ōsaka City, and Nerima Ward. The government assumed that this event would enlighten people about the attractiveness of urban agriculture. A host of the event wished people to realize that many urban areas enjoyed agricultural products and purchase vegetables grown in urbanized areas (Japan Broadcasting Corporation, November 19, 2023 [https://www3.nhk.or.jp/shutoken-news/20231119/1000099295.html]).

Urbanized cities have limited farmland because residential, commercial, and industrial districts occupy large areas. However, urban residents wish to maintain agriculture and farmland in urban areas. A survey of city residents in Three Major Metropolitan Areas (*San dai toshi ken*) in Japan was conducted in October 2023. The results revealed that 35.9% of the respondents stated that urban agriculture and farmland should be preserved by all means, and 35.8% stated that agriculture and farmland in urbanized areas should be maintained rather than disposed of. Specifically, 71.7% of urban residents wish to sustain agriculture and farmland in urban areas [4].

Urban residents' responses to other questions in the same survey implied that they were interested in agricultural practices and wished to purchase agricultural products cultivated in their residential areas. Of all the respondents, only 4.4% had been engaged in agricultural work on civic farmlands (*shimin nōen*), which compose many plots in urban areas for residents to rent and enjoy agriculture as a hobby, or on experience farmlands (*taiken nōen*) for non-farmers to experience agricultural work. However, 56.0% of the respondents who had not been engaged in agriculture on civic or experience farmlands were interested in agricultural work on these types of farmland. Moreover, 19.1% of the respondents in urban areas had purchased agricultural products cultivated in their neighborhoods, and 48.4% wanted to purchase those agricultural products [4].

The survey asked urban residents how their municipal governments should use vacant land in urban areas. The results revealed that 23.7% of the respondents were eager to convert vacant land into farmland, and 37.5% preferred transforming vacant land to farmland rather than doing nothing. Therefore, 61.2% of respondents wished to convert vacant land into farmland in urban areas [4].

As of October 1, 2020, the population of 11 cities in Japan exceeded one million (The Ministry of Internal Affairs and Communications, July 5, 2022 [https://www.soumu.go.jp/main_sosiki/jichi_gyousei/bunken/shitei_toshi-ichiran.html]). All of these cities are ordinance-designated cities (*seirei shitei toshi*) whose governments assume most of the charge of prefectural governments in addition to the charge of city governments. Except for Kawasaki City, these large cities are prefectural capitals that play significant roles in the politics and economics of their respective prefectures.

Table 1. Population and prefectural capital

Rank	City	Population (as of October 1, 2020)	Prefectural capital
1	Yokohama	3,777,491	Kanagawa Prefecture
2	Ōsaka	2,752,412	Ōsaka Prefecture
3	Nagoya	2,332,176	Aichi Prefecture
4	Sapporo	1,973,395	Hokkaidō Prefecture
5	Fukuoka	1,612,392	Fukuoka Prefecture
6	Kawasaki	1,538,262	-
7	Kōbe	1,525,152	Hyōgo Prefecture
8	Kyōto	1,463,723	Kyōto Prefecture
9	Saitama	1,324,025	Saitama Prefecture
10	Hiroshima	1,200,754	Hiroshima Prefecture
11	Sendai	1,096,704	Miyagi Prefecture

Source: Data on the population of cities were obtained from the census conducted by the Ministry of Internal Affairs and Communications. [https://www.e-stat.go.jp/stat-search/files?page=1&layout=datalist&toukei=00200521&tstat=000001136464&cycle=0&tclass1=000001136466&stat_infid=000032142402&tclass2val=0].

Large cities tend to cultivate vegetables to supply urban consumers with fresh products. Regarding value, the proportion of vegetables in all agricultural products was 24% in the entire area of Japan in 2021. However, in the same year, Yokohama, Nagoya, and Ōsaka Cities, the representative large cities in Three Major Metropolitan Areas of Japan, enjoyed higher percentages of vegetables, 60%, 54%, and 80%, respectively [4]. Large cities can use their features as places that hold many residents, that is, many food consumers who wish fresh vegetables to be cultivated in their living areas.

Several large city governments have implemented urban agriculture programs in novel ways. For example, in Kōbe City, farmers' markets are held with collaboration among farmers, city government officials, young people, and university students. Farmers' markets aim to stimulate the young generation's interest in agriculture to counter the aging of agricultural workers [4].

Another way of the Kōbe City Government to further agriculture is to establish farmland in a park. The city government decided to renovate the park because few people visited it, and the city government was willing to provide citizens with opportunities to interact with agricultural workers [11].

The Fukuoka City Government founded a park where citizens engaged in agricultural work. Farmers working on farmland around the park instruct citizens to cultivate and harvest agricultural products [6].

In 1995, the Sapporo City Government established a site to promote citizens' agricultural experiences and interactions with agricultural workers. This site comprises zones for interaction, cultivation, dairy farming, and so on. Visitors use the farmland for experiences or rent, enjoy a horse ranch for children, visit restaurants, and ride on horse-drawn carriages at the site. Farmers' markets and harvest festivals are held for visitors to purchase local agricultural products. Visitors can make butter, sausages, ice cream, and *soba* noodles by hand [12].

Moreover, the Sapporo City Government assists owners of strawberry fields and confectionery shops by holding strawberry fairs. This event is an opportunity for citizens to purchase strawberries and cakes made from strawberries and other agricultural products cultivated in Sapporo City [12].

Another contribution of the Sapporo City Government toward the progress of agriculture is to hold a competition for cakes that citizens make from fruits harvested in Sapporo City. Competition judges are the owners of strawberry fields and confectionery shops. This event promotes the formation of networks among citizens, agricultural workers, and confectioners [12].

The Kawasaki City Government in Kanagawa Prefecture introduced a program to collect volunteers to aid farmers. According to the results of interviews with 12 farmers who accepted agricultural volunteers working on their farms through the program, all the interviewees considered that the volunteers worked hard, and nine (75%) of the interviewees stated that the volunteers were eager in their agricultural work [3].

A social welfare corporation provides people with disability with opportunities to work on farmland and interact with local residents to sell agricultural products harvested by people with disability. As volunteers, local residents assist workers with disability in cultivating agricultural products. The Kawasaki City Government arranged for a collaboration between the social welfare corporation and supermarkets or hotels to promote compost production by workers with disability [13].

In 1997, the Kawasaki City Government embarked on a program to register farmland used for emergency evacuation sites. Farmland owners voluntarily register their farmland as emergency evacuation sites that evacuees can use to stay and live in after natural disasters [9].

The Yokohama City Government, located in Kanagawa Prefecture, similar to the Kawasaki City Government, also contracts farmland owners to use their farmland as emergency evacuation sites to save citizens from natural disasters, such as devastating earthquakes. The Yokohama City Government was the pioneering municipal government in using these contracts with farmers and commenced this program in 1995 [9].

In addition to the Kawasaki City Government, the Yokohama City Government implements a program of inviting volunteers and dispatching them to farmland to deal with manpower shortages in agriculture. The city government manages training courses for people who have not experienced agricultural work to engage themselves in volunteer work on farmland [8].

Some large cities may influence the municipalities around them in terms of agriculture, because they occupy superior positions of agricultural production in their prefectures. Yokohama and Kyōto are the large cities that enjoy the highest positions in the rank of agricultural outturn in their prefectures.

Table 2. Top-five municipalities in Kanagawa, Kyōto, Hyōgo Prefectures with regard to agricultural outturn

Rank	Kanagawa Prefecture		Kyōto Prefecture	
	Municipality	Agricultural outturn (10 million yen in 2022)	Municipality	Agricultural outturn (10 million yen in 2022)
1	Yokohama City	1,212	Kyōto City	903
2	Miura City	982	Kyōtango City	878
3	Fujisawa City	581	Fukuchiyama City	654
4	Odawara City	381	Kameoka City	634
5	Kawasaki City	374	Kyōtamba Town	626

Rank	Hyōgo Prefecture	
	Municipality	Agricultural outturn (10 million yen in 2022)
1	Minamiawaji City	2,502
2	Kōbe City	1,356
3	Tamba City	1,206
4	Toyooka City	1,120
5	Kamigōri Town	721

Source: Data on agricultural outturn in municipalities were obtained from an inquiry conducted by the Ministry of Agriculture, Forestry and Fisheries. [https://www.e-stat.go.jp/stat-search/files?page=1&layout=datalist&toukei=00500249&tstat=000001108355&cycle=7&year=20220&month=0&tclass1=000001108375&tclass2=000001215267].

Yokohama City surpassed Kyōto City in the outturn of agriculture in 2022: 12,120 million yen for Yokohama City and 9,030 million yen for Kyōto City. Kōbe City is the only large city that exceeded Yokohama City in the 2022 agricultural outturn. However, Kōbe City is not the foremost municipality in Hyōgo Prefecture with regard to agricultural outturn. In this sense, Kōbe City is not the central municipality in agriculture of the prefecture.

Table 3. Agricultural outturn in large cities

Rank	Large city	Agricultural outturn (10 million yen in 2022)	Rank	Large city	Agricultural outturn (10 million yen in 2022)
1	Kōbe	1,356	7	Sendai	603
2	Yokohama	1,212	8	Sapporo	601
3	Saitama	957	9	Kawasaki	374
4	Kyōto	903	10	Nagoya	240
5	Hiroshima	628	11	Ōsaka	53
6	Fukuoka	615			

Source: Data on agricultural outturn in municipalities were obtained from an inquiry conducted by the Ministry of Agriculture, Forestry and Fisheries. [https://www.e-stat.go.jp/stat-search/files?page=1&layout=datalist&toukei=00500249&tstat=000001108355&cycle=7&year=20220&month=0&tclass1=000001108375&tclass2=000001215267].

The Yokohama City Government's programs for farmland and agriculture may have evolved agriculture and brought about the leading position of the city in the agricultural outturn within Kanagawa Prefecture. Why is agriculture prosperous in Yokohama City? This study addresses this question by focusing on the Yokohama City Government's organizations and officials in charge of farmland and agriculture.

2. Methodology

The Yokohama City Government's agricultural programs attach importance to maintaining farmland against the expansion of residential, commercial, and industrial areas. Previous studies have clarified the city government's farmland policies.

In 2009, the Yokohama City Government devised the Plan for Extending Green Zones in Yokohama (PEGZY, *Yokohama midori appu keikaku*). This plan had policies to preserve and create forests and fields, and create opportunities for citizens to become familiar with agriculture. Subsequently, the city government formed Yokohama Urban Agriculture Advancement Plan (YUAAP, *Yokohama toshi nōgyō suishin puran*), a plan specializing in agriculture and farmland rather than green zones in a broad sense, to apply to concrete and detailed agricultural programs in FY 2014 and following FYs. YUAAP adopted the PEGZY policy on opportunities for citizens to interact with the agricultural sector. Programs following these plans have been conducted with an object tax, Yokohama Green Tax (*Yokohama midori zei*), as a revenue source for the plans [1] [2] [7] [9] [10] [16] [17].

PEGZY of FY 2009 covered five years, from FY 2009 to FY 2013, followed by five-year plans after it completed its implementation period. PEGZY of FY 2009 and its successors aimed to preserve and establish places where citizens could become familiar with agriculture. PEGZY of FY 2009 established three strategies: (1) preserving forests, (2) maintaining farmland, and (3) creating green zones. Concrete measures for the second strategy included programs to preserve rural landscapes and paddy fields, establish parks containing civic farmlands, and found civic farmlands using farmland where agricultural workers cannot be secured. The plans to succeed PEGZY of FY 2009 followed the strategies and programs of their predecessor. The Environmental Planning Bureau (EPB, *Kankyō sōzō kyoku*) of the Yokohama City Government assumed charge of implementing PEGZY [1] [2] [7] [9] [14] [15] [16] [17]. Regarding departments, subordinate organizations of a bureau in the Yokohama City Government, the Green-Zone Advancement Department (*Midori appu suishin bu*) and the Agriculture Department (*Nōsei bu*) in the EPB were responsible for implementing programs of PEGZY and YUAAP, respectively [18] [19]. The EPB was created in FY 2005 and, in FY 2024, reorganized into the Green Environment Bureau (*Midori kankyō kyoku*), which undertakes PEGZY and YUAAP and does not assume sewerage programs that the EPB conducted. Previous studies on PEGZY and YUAAP indicated these plans' effectiveness for preserving farmland [7] [9] [10].

Features of PEGZY and YUAAP in terms of agricultural advancement aim to increase civic farmlands and transform farmland abandoned by its owners owning to aging or lack of agricultural workers into civic farmlands. In particular, the conversion of abandoned farmland into parks containing civic farmlands is noteworthy because few municipal governments have implemented it [2].

Yokohama City has many civic farmlands. The Ministry of Agriculture, Forestry and Fisheries (MAFF) divides Japan into nine regions and checks the number of civic farmlands in each region. On March 31, 2023, Kantō Region held the most civic farmlands and was followed by Kinki Region. Top-two prefectures in each region were Kanagawa Prefecture and Tōkyō Metropolis in Kantō Region and Hyōgo and Kyōto Prefectures in Kinki Region. Yokohama City had the most civic farmlands among the top-five municipalities in each prefecture.

Table 4. The numbers of civic farmlands in the regions as of March 31, 2023

Rank	Region	Number of civic farmlands (as of March 31, 2023)	Rank	Region	Number of civic farmlands (as of March 31, 2023)
1	Kantō	2,289	6	Hokuriku	132
2	Kinki	640	7	Tōhoku	106
3	Tōkai	520	8	Hokkaidō	98
4	Chūgoku Shikoku	321	9	Okinawa	18
5	Kyūshū	184			

Source: Data were obtained from an inquiry conducted by the Ministry of Agriculture, Forestry and Fisheries. [https://www.maff.go.jp/j/nousin/kouryu/tosi_nougyo/attach/pdf/s_joukyou-2.pdf].

Table 5. The numbers of civic farmlands in the prefectures of Kantō and Kinki Regions as of March 31, 2023

	Kantō Region			Kinki Region	
Rank	Prefecture	Number of civic farmlands (as of March 31, 2023)	Rank	Prefecture	Number of civic farmlands (as of March 31, 2023)
1	Kanagawa	727	1	Hyōgo	105
2	Tōkyō	499	2	Kyōto	50
3	Nagano	324	3	Ōsaka	44
4	Saitama	252	4	Nara	24
5	Shizuoka	117	5	Shiga	10
6	Chiba	103	6	Wakayama	9
7	Ibaraki	85			
8	Yamanashi	77			
9	Gumma	75			
10	Tochigi	30			

Sources: Data were obtained from inquiries conducted by Kanto and Kinki Regional Agricultural Administration Offices (*Kantō nōsei kyoku* and *Kinki nōsei kyoku*) of the Ministry of Agriculture, Forestry and Fisheries. [https://www.maff.go.jp/kanto/nouson/shinkou/nouen/attach/pdf/index-4.pdf]. [https://www.maff.go.jp/kinki/keikaku/tosizyumin/simin_nouen.html].

Table 6. Top-five municipalities in Kanagawa, Hyōgo, and Kyōto Prefectures and Tōkyō Metropolis in terms of the number of civic farmlands

\multicolumn{5}{c}{Kantō Region}				
\multicolumn{2}{c}{Kanagawa Prefecture}		\multicolumn{2}{c}{Tōkyō Metropolis}	
Rank	Municipality	Number of civic farmlands (as of March 31, 2023)	Rank	Municipality	Number of civic farmlands (as of March 31, 2023)
1	Yokohama City	285	1	Nerima Ward	52
2	Sagamihara City	75	2	Hachiōji City	38
3	Chigasaki Cty	62	3	Edogawa Ward	31
4	Kawasaki City	57	4	Itabashi Ward	29
5	Hadano City	45	5	Oume City	24

\multicolumn{6}{c}{Kinki Region}					
\multicolumn{3}{c}{Hyōgo Prefecture}			\multicolumn{3}{c}{Kyōto Prefecture}		
Rank	Municipality	Number of civic farmlands (as of March 31, 2023)	Rank	Municipality	Number of civic farmlands (as of March 31, 2023)
1	Itami City	25	1	Kyōto City	13
2	Nishinomiya City	10	2	Jōyō City	9
3	Tambasasayama City	6	3	Kameoka City	7
3	Taishi Town	6	4	Nagaokakyō City	4
5	Takarazuka City	5	4	Kizugawa City	4
5	Kawanishi City	5			
5	Asago City	5			

Sources: Data were obtained from inquiries conducted by Kanagawa Prefectural Government, Tōkyō Metropolitan Government, and Kinki Regional Agricultural Administration Office (*Kinki nōsei kyoku*) of the Ministry of Agriculture, Forestry and Fisheries. [https://www.pref.kanagawa.jp/documents/3946/siminnouenr5_3.pdf]. [https://www.agri.metro.tokyo.lg.jp/files/shimin/R5shimin.pdf]. [https://www.maff.go.jp/kinki/keikaku/tosizyumin/simin_nouen.html].

As indicated by the previous studies, PEGZY and YUAAP may have contributed to preserving farmland by transforming abandoned farmland into civic farmlands and parks containing civic farmlands in Yokohama City. However, the ability to implement programs in accordance with PEGZY and YUAAP is also a significant factor in increasing civic farmlands. The EPB undertook programs to establish civic farmlands. This study aims to clarify the features of EPB departments, the largest organizational unit within the bureau, and officials undertaking PEGZY and agriculture, including YUAAP, in the EPB. The officials discussed in this study are those who held the designations of the Director General for Green-Zone Program Advancement (*Midori seisaku suishin tantō riji*), the Director General for Green-Zone Advancement (*Midori appu suishin tantō riji*), the Executive Director of the Green-Zone Advancement Department (*Midori appu suishin buchō*), and the Executive Director of the Agriculture Department (*Nōsei buchō* or *Nōsei tantō buchō*). In the Yokohama City Government, a director general for a certain program (*riji*) is the highest position under a director general of a bureau (*kyokuchō*). The bureau has several departments (*bu*) comprising multiple divisions (*ka*). These four positions were highly ranked among the positions in charge of PEGZY and agriculture, covering YUAAP, within the EPB.

This study ascertains the career paths of EPB officials who held high-ranked positions between FY 2014 and FY 2023. The EPB was established in FY 2005, continued until FY 2023, and was reorganized in FY 2024. The second half of the EPB's existence period may enjoy regular patterns of officials' career paths, whereas the first half may use trial and error to identify ways to manage EPB personnel. The second and third versions of PEGZY cover the periods from FY 2014 to FY 2018 and from FY 2019 to FY 2023, respectively. Many officials who held high-ranked positions concerning green zones and agriculture in or before FY 2013 also held division-director positions in or before FY 2004. Therefore, these officials' career paths at the division-director level or higher do not necessarily signify career paths in the EPB.

The departments in the EPB and career paths of officials obtaining the four high-ranked positions aforementioned were ascertained with *Shokuinroku: Gekan* (List of Personnel: The Second Volume) edited by the National Printing Bureau or the Printing Bureau of the Ministry of Finance. *Yokohama shi shokuinroku* (List of Personnel in the Yokohama City Government), edited by the Yokohama City Government compensated for some FY 2012 data, which *Shokuinroku: Gekan* lacks. From FY 2014 to FY 2023, the EPB contained departments of general affairs, the environment, preservation/extension of green zones, agriculture, parks, and sewerage. Three officials who held high ranked positions concerned with green-zone maintenance/expansion and agriculture from FY 2014 to FY 2023 held division-director-level positions in the bureau of green zones, agriculture, and parks (*Ryokusei kyoku*) before the EPB was established in FY 2005. This bureau did not include the departments of environmental preservation (*Kankyō hozen kyoku*) and sewerage (*Gesuidō kyoku*), which the EPB contained. This study excluded the years when the officials held division-director-level positions in the departments of green zones, agriculture, parks, environment, and sewerage in or before FY 2004 and displayed these years for reference in the table.

3. Results

Table 7 displays the departments of the EPB. The period during which the EPB existed was divided into four parts. In all parts, the EPB held the Environmental Preservation Department. In and after FY 2009, when PEGZY commenced operations, the Green-Zone Advancement Department was located in the EPB. The Executive Director of the Agriculture Department was placed in the Environmental Activity Advancement Department (*Kankyō katsudō suishin bu*) from FY 2005 to FY 2008, the Green-Zone Advancement Department from FY 2009 to FY 2019, and the Agriculture Department from FY 2020 to FY 2023. Programs concerning parks were undertaken by the Environmental Activity Advancement Department and the Environmental Facilities Department (*Kankyō shisetsu bu*) from FY 2005 to 2008 and the Green-Zone Advancement Department from FY 2009 to FY 2023. Management of sewerage was conducted by the Environmental Arrangement Department (*Kankyō seibi bu*) from FY 2005 to FY 2010 and the Sewerage Plan Coordination Department (*Gesuidō keikaku chōsei bu*), the Sewerage Pipeline Department (*Gesuidō kanro bu*), and the Sewerage Facilities Department (*Gesuidō shisetsu bu*) from FY 2011 to FY 2023. As a single bureau, the EPB covered preservation and extension of green zones, including farmland, agriculture, the environment, parks, and sewerage.

Table 8 presents the years in which high-ranking officials held positions at the division-director level or higher in the EPB before they became director generals or executive directors undertaking green zones or agriculture. Positions in the EPB were classified as preservation and extension of green zones (PEGZY), agriculture, the environment, parks, sewerage, and general affairs. If the official positions at the division-director level or higher before the EPB was established in FY 2005 belonged to the departments undertaking green zones, agriculture, the environment, parks, and sewerage, the years for which the officials remained in the positions are displayed in parentheses in the table for reference.

Table 7. Departments in the Environmental Planning Bureau

Fiscal year	2005–2008	2009–2010	2011–2019	2020–2023
Department	General Affairs Department (*Sōmu bu*)	General Affairs Department (*Sōmu bu*)	Policy Coordination Department (*Seisaku chōsei bu*)	Policy Coordination Department (*Seisaku chōsei bu*)
	Comprehensive Planning Department (*Sōgō kikaku bu*)	Planning Department (*Kikaku bu*)	General Affairs Department (*Sōmu bu*)	General Affairs Department (*Sōmu bu*)
	Environmental Preservation Department (*Kankyō hozen bu*)	Green-Zone Advancement Department (*Midori appu suishin bu*) *Executive Director of Agriculture Department (*Nōsei tantō buchō*) was assigned to this department.	Environmental Preservation Department (*Kankyō hozen bu*)	Environmental Preservation Department (*Kankyō hozen bu*)
	Environmental Activity Advancement Department (*Kankyō katsudō suishin bu*) *Executive Director of Agriculture Department (*Nōsei tantō buchō*) was assigned to this department.	Environmental Preservation Department (*Kankyō hozen bu*)	Green-Zone Advancement Department (*Midori appu suishin bu*) *Executive Director of Agriculture Department (*Nōsei tantō buchō*) was assigned to this department.	Green-Zone Advancement Department (*Midori appu suishin bu*)
	Environmental Facilities Department (*Kankyō shisetsu bu*)	Facilities Management Department (*Shisetsu kanri bu*)	Park and Greening Department (*Kōen ryokuchi bu*)	Agriculture Department (*Nōsei bu*)
	Environmental Arrangement Department (*Kankyō seibi bu*)	Environmental Arrangement Department (*Kankyō seibi bu*)	Sewerage Plan Coordination Department (*Gesuidō keikaku chōsei bu*)	Park and Greening Department (*Kōen ryokuchi bu*)

Fiscal year	2005–2008	2009–2010	2011–2019	2020–2023
Department			Sewerage Pipeline Department (*Gesuidō kanro bu*) Sewerage Facilities Department (*Gesuidō shisetsu bu*)	Sewerage Plan Coordination Department (*Gesuidō keikaku chōsei bu*) Sewerage Pipeline Department (*Gesuidō kanro bu*) Sewerage Facilities Department (*Gesuidō shisetsu bu*)

Sources: Data were obtained from *Shokuinroku: Gekan* edited by the National Printing Bureau and *Yokohama shi shokuinroku: Heisei 24 nen ban* edited by the Yokohama City Government.

Table 8. Years in which officials held positions at the division-director level or higher in fields undertaken by the Environmental Planning Bureau before they reached the positions of director generals or executive directors

Director General for Green-Zone Program Advancement (*Midori seisaku suishin tantō riji*)						
Period of Director General for Green-Zone Program Advancement (fiscal year)	Years in positions at division-director level or higher in Environmental Planning Bureau before Director General for Green-Zone Program Advancement					
	General affairs	Environment	Preservation and extension of green zones (PEGZY)	Agriculture	Park	Sewerage
2023	0	0	3	0	10	0

Director General for Green-Zone Advancement (*Midori appu suishin tantō riji*)						
Period of Director General for Green-Zone Advancement (fiscal year)	Years in positions at division-director level or higher in Environmental Planning Bureau before Director General for Green-Zone Advancement					
	General affairs	Environment	Preservation and extension of green zones (PEGZY)	Agriculture	Park	Sewerage
2017–2022	0	3	3	0	4 (4)	0
2016	0	0	5	0	6	0
2014–2015	0	4	5 (1)	0 (2)	0	0

Executive Director of Green-Zone Advancement Department (*Midori appu suishin buchō*)						
Period of Executive Director of Green-Zone Advancement Department (fiscal year)	Years in positions at division-director level or higher in Environmental Planning Bureau before Executive Director of Green-Zone Advancement Department					
	General affairs	Environment	Preservation and extension of green zones (PEGZY)	Agriculture	Park	Sewerage
2023	0	0	10	2	7	0
2021–2022	0	0	3	0	5	0
2020	0	0	5	0	0	0
2016–2019	3	0	0	2	0	0
2014–2015	0	0	3	0	6	0

Executive Director of Agriculture Department (*Nōsei buchō* or *Nōsei tantō buchō*)						
Period of Executive Director of Agriculture Department (fiscal year)	Years in positions at division-director level or higher in Environmental Planning Bureau before Executive Director of Agriculture Department					
	General affairs	Environment	Preservation and extension of green zones (PEGZY)	Agriculture	Park	Sewerage
2021–2023	0	0	0	4	0	0
2019–2020	0	4	0	0	3	0
2016–2018	0	0	2	0	3 (1)	0
2014–2015	3	0	0	0	0	0

Note: The numbers in parentheses indicate the years in which officials held positions at the division-director level or higher before the Environmental Planning Bureau was

established in FY 2005.
Sources: Data were obtained from *Shokuinroku: Gekan* edited by the National Printing Bureau or the Printing Bureau of the Ministry of Finance and *Yokohama shi shokuinroku: Heisei 24 nen ban* edited by the Yokohama City Government.

    The Executive Director of the Agriculture Department and the directors of the divisions concerned with agriculture were incorporated into the Environmental Activity Advancement Department from FY 2005 to FY 2008, and the Green-Zone Advancement Department from FY 2009 to FY 2019. Therefore, the positions were classified into agriculture or green zones based on the positions' fields rather than the departments to which the positions belonged. The Director of Environmental Activity Support Center (*Kankyō katsudō shien sentā*) in the EPB is a division-director-level position. This center undertakes programs concerned with green zones, agriculture, and parks. Therefore, the Director of the center is regarded as responsible for these three fields. The EPB dispatched officials to Yokohama Greenery Foundation (*Yokohama shi midori no kyōkai*), which implements programs to advance green zones and manage parks. Officials assigned to this foundation are considered holding positions concerning both green zones and parks. The EPB's officials dispatched to Yokohama Sport Association (*Yokohama shi supōtsu kyōkai*) are regarded as provided with a position pertaining to parks because fields for sports are regarded as a type of park in the EPB. From FY 2005 to FY 2008, division-director-level positions responsible for the Plan of Water and Green Zones in Yokohama City (*Yokohama shi mizu to midori no kihon keikaku*) were established in the Environmental Equipment Department of the EPB. This plan covered green zones and parks. The division-director-level or higher positions in charge of the plan are regarded as undertaking green zones and parks.

    Among the officials who held the four high-ranked positions concerned with the preservation and extension of green zones, one official held only green-zone positions at the division-director level or higher before reaching the high-ranked positions of green zones. Other high-ranking officials in the field of green zones held positions concerned with general affairs, the environment, agriculture, and parks. The EPB tended to provide its high-ranking officials responsible for green zones with opportunities to work in multiple fields rather than specializing in a single field of green zones.

    Officials assigned to the Executive Director of the Agriculture Department tended not to experience positions concerned with agriculture before reaching the position of Executive Director. Of the four officials, a single official held only agricultural positions at the division-director level or higher. The remaining three officials held positions of fields other than agriculture. The Executive Director of the Agriculture Department could consider agricultural matters from the viewpoint of other fields, rather from an exclusive standpoint of agriculture.

The high-ranking officials responsible for green zones and agriculture did not hold sewerage positions at the division-director level or higher. Although the EPB united, with regard to personnel, the fields of green zones, agriculture, the environment, and parks, the departments in charge of sewerage were estranged from other departments in the EPB.

4. Discussion

Regarding internal organizations, the EPB contained the fields of green zones, agriculture, the environment, parks, and sewerage. The bureau could handle programs for green zones or agriculture associated with other fields, such as environmental protection and relaxation in parks.

Regarding personnel, specialists exclusive to green zones or agriculture were not always assigned to high-ranked positions concerned with green zones or agriculture in the EPB. Officials with experience in other fields, such as the environment and parks, tended to hold high-ranked positions responsible for green zones and agriculture. This tendency may have influenced the EPB's operations of programs concerned with civic farmland in terms of personnel. Although the EPB contained departments of sewerage, it did not tend to connect the experiences of positions responsible for sewerage with the high-ranked positions in charge of green zones and agriculture.

A feature of the EPB's internal organizations and positions concerned with green zones and agriculture is that these organizations and positions could accept the influence of other fields, such as the environment and parks. This organizational and personnel arrangement in the fields of farmland and agriculture presumes that farmland and agriculture contribute to environmental protection and citizens' relaxation.

Many people in Yokohama City share the view that farmland or agriculture coexists with the environment and relaxation. The Yokohama City Government implemented a survey of people's opinions on civic farmlands from October to November 2022. The respondents included 730 residents, three workers in workplaces, and one student at a school in the city. Among the respondents, 71.7% selected the response, "Good," to the question, "What do you think about a life with a civic farmland close to you?" The questionnaire asked respondents who answered "Good" to the previous question about why they thought so (a multiple-choice question). Most respondents (78.1%) selected the answer "Because I can become familiar with agriculture and green areas." The response with the second highest percentage (34.0%) was "Because I use or want to use a civic farmland" (https://www.city.yokohama.lg.jp/city-info/koho-kocho/kocho/e_anke-to/kekka/R04kekka.files/0098_20221219.pdf). These responses signify that, regardless of whether people in Yokohama City are engaged in farmland agriculture, they regard farmland as providing them with positive emotions. Farmland may be considered places for not only economic activity but also calmness and relaxation.

5. Conclusion

This study reveals the features of the Yokohama City Government's organizations and personnel in the fields of green zones and agriculture. The EPB, established in FY 2005 and reorganized in FY 2024, assumed charge of green zones, including civic farmland, agriculture, the environment, parks, and sewerage. As a single bureau, the EPB implemented programs concerning not only farmland and agriculture, but also those concerning the environment and parks. The EPB could mingle these fields and conduct programs on civic farmlands and agriculture by connecting them with matters of the environment or relaxation. The general and executive directors in charge of green zones and agriculture in the EPB tended to experience division-director-level or higher positions in other fields that the EPB undertook. High-ranking EPB officials responsible for green zones or agriculture with experience in division-director-level or higher positions in the fields of only green zones or agriculture were uncommon.

As MAFF states, agricultural workers continue to decrease in number and increase in average age [5]. A municipal government, particularly in an urbanized area, is confronted with difficulty in establishing a bureau specializing in the field of agriculture or farmland, because agriculture is an industry that is declining in Japan and tends to be regarded as an insignificant field. An alternative to establishing a bureau specializing in agriculture or farmland is to organize a bureau in charge of the economy, including agriculture, and the department and divisions responsible for agriculture as an internal organization of the bureau. According to the National Printing Bureau's *Shokuinroku: Gekan* that presents organizations and personnel in municipal governments in FY 2023, bureaus in charge of the economy contained departments or divisions of agriculture in the large city governments of Sapporo, Sendai, Saitama, Kawasaki, Kyōto, Ōsaka, Kōbe, and Hiroshima.

A feature of Yokohama City Government organizations and personnel in farmland and agricultural fields is their combination with the environment or parks. Agriculture is related to the environmental comfort and relaxation of parks for city residents. This technique implies the reverse direction of specialization. In general, the specialization of a municipal government's internal organizations and personnel in a certain field may be expected to bring about exhaustive implementation of detailed programs. However, in combination with other fields, the organizations and personnel of a municipal government can provide fields of farmland and agriculture with additional meaning and novel value.

References (The websites were finally accessed on September 26, 2024.)

[1] Enari, Takashi. 2017, "Yokohama shi no toshi nōgyō to nōchi hozen [Urban Agriculture and Farmland Conservation in Yokohama City]." *Suido no chi: Nōgyō nōson kōgakkai shi.* [*Water, Land and Environmental Engineering: Journal of the Japanese Society of Irrigation, Drainage and Rural Engineering*]. 85 (7): 639–643.

[2] Kawakami, Jun and Tōru Terada. 2019, "Bunkuen o setchi shita toshi kōen no kūkan oyobi unei jō no tokuchō ni kansuru kōsatsu [A Discussion on the Spatial Features and Management Systems in Allotment Gardens in Urban Park]." *Randosukēpu kenkyū* [*Journal of the Japanese Institute of Landscape Architecture*]. 82 (5): 543–46.

[3] Kitagawa, Mizuki and Toshihiro Hattori. 2014, "Toshi nōgyō no ninaite to shite no ennō borantia no yakuwari [The Role of the Volunteer for Supporting Farming as a Bearer of an Urban Agriculture Land]." *Suido no chi: Nōgyō nōson kōgakkai shi* [*Water, Land and Environmental Engineering: Journal of the Japanese Society of Irrigation, Drainage and Rural Engineering*]. 82 (2): 115–18.

[4] The Ministry of Agriculture, Forestry and Fisheries (MAFF). 2024, "Toshi nōgyō o meguru jōsei ni tsuite." [https://www.maff.go.jp/j/nousin/kouryu/tosi_nougyo/attach/pdf/t_kuwashiku-54.pdf].

[5] The Ministry of Agriculture, Forestry and Fisheries (MAFF). 2024, *Reiwa 5 nendo shokuryō, nōgyō, nōson hakusho*. [https://www.maff.go.jp/j/wpaper/w_maff/r5/pdf/zentaiban.pdf].

[6] The Ministry of Land, Infrastructure, Transport and Tourism (MLIT). 2019, "Toshi to midori, nō ga kyōsei suru machizukuri yūryō torikumi jirei shū." [https://www.mlit.go.jp/common/001341508.pdf].

[7] Naitō, Kōhei. 2010, "'Yokohama midori appu keikaku' to 'Yokohama midori zei': Midori no hozen, sōzō e muketa aratana torikumi ['Yokohama Greenery Promotion Plan' and 'Yokohama Green Tax': New Policy for Greenery Preservation and Creation]." *Keikaku gyōsei* [*Planning Administration*]. 33 (2): 59–62.

[8] Satō, Tadayasu. 2017, "Toshi nōgyō ni okeru ennō katsuyō nōka ni motomerareru yōken: Kanagawa kennai o jirei to shite [Requirements for Farmers Using Volunteer Workers in Urban Agriculture: A Case Study in Kanagawa Prefecture]." *Kanagawa ken nōgyō gijutsu sentā kenkyū hōkoku* [*Bulletin of the Kanagawa Agricultural Technology Center*]. (161): 25–34.

[9] Seki, Tatsuya. 2014, "Kokoro yasuragu ryokuchi kūkan: Toshi nōgyō no tokuchō to kadai, Yokohama, Kawasaki chiiki [Everyone's State of Mind on Green Tract of Land Space]." *Kikaika nōgyō* [*Farming Mechanization*]. (3163): 5–10.

[10] Shimizu, Kazuaki. 2022, "Tōkei kara mita Yokohama shi no nōgyō no chiiki teki tokuchō [Regional Characteristics of Yokohama's Agriculture Based on Statistics]." *Jimbungaku kenkyūsho hō* [*Bulletin of the Institute for Humanities Research*]. (68): 73–83.

[11] Shimpo, Naomi. 2021, "Nō o tsūjita toshi kōen to chiiki komyuniti no saisei: Hyōgo ken Kōbe shi no Hirano kōpu nōen no jirei kara [Revitalization of Park and Local Community through an Urban Gardening Project: A Case Study on Hirano Coop Nouen in Kobe, Hyogo]." *Toshi keikaku hōkoku shū* [*Reports of the City Planning Institute of Japan*]. (20): 154–56.

[12] Teramoto, Chinao. 2004, "Sapporo shi ni okeru toshi gata nōgyō no tenkai: Sapporo toretatekko jigyō, Sapporo satorando, Sapporo nōgakkō [The Development of City Agriculture in Sapporo City: Project of the Sapporotoretatekko, Sapporo Satorando, Sapporo College of Agriculture]." *Journal of Environmental Science Laboratory*. (11): 47–71.

[13] Tokuda, Kenji and Chunxia Li. 2019, "Toshi seisaku ni okeru nōgyō inobēshon no jikkō sei: Kawasaki shi no jirei kenkyū ni motozuku kōsatsu [Effectiveness of Agricultural Innovation in Urban Policy: Consideration on Case Studies in Kawasaki City]." *Senshū keizaigaku ronshū* [*Economic Bulletin of Senshu University*]. 54 (2): 23–118.

[14] Tsutaya, Eiichi. 2015, "Toshi nōgyō ga motsu shakai dezain nōryoku hakki to iu igi." *Gekkan JA*. 61 (8): 26–29.

[15] Yokohama City Government. 2009, "Yokohama midori appu keikaku (Shinki, kakujū shisaku)." [https://www.city.yokohama.lg.jp/kurashi/machizukuri-kankyo/midori-koen/midori_up/kako/about-midoriup.files/0010_20180828.pdf].

[16] Yokohama City Government. 2020, "Yokohama no nōgyō: Gaiyō, shisaku no ayumi, nōgyō tōkei hoka." [https://www.city.yokohama.lg.jp/kurashi/machizukuri-kankyo/nochi/nougyou/sesaku/nousei.files/0041_20201223.pdf].

[17] Yokohama City Government. 2022, "Yokohama shi ni okeru 'nōen tsuki kōen' no seibi ni tsuite." *Tochi sōgō kenkyū*. 30 (1): 37–43.

[18] Yokohama City Government. 2022, "Yokohama toshi nōgyō suishin puran 2019–2023 no shinchoku jōkyō: Reiwa 4 nendo ban." [https://www.city.yokohama.lg.jp/kurashi/machizukuri-kankyo/nochi/nougyou/nougyousuishinplan.files/0043_20231204.pdf].

[19] Yokohama City Government. 2023, "Yokohama midori appu keikaku [2019–2023]: 4 ka nen (2019 nendo–2022 nendo) no jigyō, torikumi no hyōka, kenshō." [https://www.city.yokohama.lg.jp/kurashi/machizukuri-kankyo/midori-koen/midori_up/jigyou_houkoku.files/0042_20231016.pdf].

Chapter 2

Negative Externality and Green Technology Adoption in Oligopolistic Markets

Hiroki Iwata

Faculty of Human Environmental Studies, Hiroshima-shudo University
1-1-1,Ozuka-higashi, Asaminami-ku, Hiroshima, 731-3195, JAPAN

Abstract

This paper analyzes the technology choices of firms in oligopolistic markets using a two-stage game model. First, firms choose between production technologies that involve negative externalities and green technologies, followed by either quantity or price competition. In addition, this study examines a situation where the negative externalities generated by firms affect their production costs. This is a situation in which not only negative externalities arising from the firm's own actions, but also negative externalities generated by other firms affect production costs. The analysis demonstrates that, when such effects are present, firms can have incentives to voluntarily adopt technology that reduces their environmental burden under Cournot competition. In contrast, under Bertrand competition, voluntary adoption of technology to reduce their environmental burden does not occur. Additionally, the introduction of an environmental tax under these circumstances has the effect of promoting the adoption of green technology in the Cournot market, but its effect would be limited in the Bertrand market.

Key Words:
Green technology, Voluntary approach, Negative Externality

1. Introduction

Environmental issues are significant social challenges, and addressing them is thought to require the adoption and dissemination of green technologies to play an important role. For instance, SDGs Goals 7, 9, 12, 13, 15, and 17 highlight the importance of adopting and promoting green technologies. These goals emphasize the role of green technology in ensuring access to affordable and clean energy (Goal 7), promoting sustainable industrialization and innovation (Goal 9), fostering sustainable consumption and production patterns (Goal 12), urgently addressing climate change (Goal 13), conserving terrestrial ecosystems (Goal 15), and strengthening partnerships for sustainable development (Goal 17). Collectively, these goals underscore the necessity of advancing green technology to achieve long-term sustainability and environmental resilience on a global scale.

From an economic standpoint, environmental problems can be viewed as a form of market failure caused by negative externalities. When firms are the source of these externalities, they lack the incentive to internalize them voluntarily. As a result, government intervention is often justified to correct the firms' behavior and restore market efficiency by implementing environmental policies.

In contrast, recent years have seen more instances where firms, without direct government intervention, choose to engage in environmentally friendly actions voluntarily[1]. In existing research, the primary motivations for firms to adopt voluntary approaches are often attributed to factors such as the presence of stakeholders who favor environmentally conscious firms and the anticipation of future environmental regulations. Notable studies on this topic include Arora and Gangopadhyay (1995), Segerson and Miceli (1998), Amacher et al. (2004), and Conrad (2005). This study examines the potential for implementing a voluntary approach under conditions different from the motivations typically considered in existing research on voluntary approaches. The situations considered in this study are as follows. When examining real-world environmental issues, the creation of negative externalities by economic agents affects not only external parties not involved in market transactions but can also impact the agents themselves. For example, when multiple firms jointly utilize a shared resource that becomes polluted through their activities, these firms not only impose environmental burdens on society but also face an increase in their own production costs. For example, this issue also arises in the context of global warming. In practice the Task Force on Climate-related Financial Disclosures (TCFD) considers how climate change affects firms' financial conditions, yet the greenhouse gases contributing to climate change are often the result of firms' production activities. In existing research, Linnenluecke et al. (2011)

---

[1] An overarching study on voluntary approaches can be found in Khanna (2001) and Segerson (2013).

analyze the impact of climate change on firm relocation. In cases where environmental damage caused by firms or other entities negatively impacts the firm itself, the question arises: how does this affect the firm's choice of technology? A theoretical analysis under such situations, at least to the best of my knowledge, has not been adequately conducted in existing research[2].

There is extensive existing research on firms' adoption of green technologies. For example, Innes and Biral (2002) explored innovations aimed at reducing environmental impacts in oligopolistic markets under uncertainty. Montero (2002a, 2002b) compared the incentives for technological development under different environmental regulations. Milliman and Prince (1989) also address the selection of pollution-reducing technologies under different policy regimes, incorporating a model that takes the innovation process into account. Furthermore, Lambertini et al. (2017) analyze technology choice in the presence of spillover effects. Lambertini et al. (2022) used a product differentiation approach to analyze the Porter Hypothesis and the effect of environmental taxes on green technology innovation. Additionally, Buccella et al. (2021) examined strategic decision-making between firms regarding the adoption of pollution-reducing technologies in response to environmental taxes.

This study analyzes decision-making regarding the choice of green technologies in situations where negative externalities impact firms' costs, using both Cournot and Bertrand market structures. First, it examines cases where technology selection is driven by a voluntary approach, aiming to clarify how negative external effects influence firms' technological decisions. This analysis reveals that, when these effects are present, a situation arises in which firms are likely to adopt a voluntary approach. Subsequently, environmental policies are introduced to demonstrate how such policies impact the adoption of green technologies.

2. The model
2.1 Assumption

Consider a market with 2 firms ($i = \{1,2\}$)[3]. In this model, there are two types of technology available to firms, denoted as $j = \{b: brown, g: green\}$. Initially, both firms are using the brown technology, and the marginal cost of production for both firms is c_b. For simplicity, assume that $c_b = 0$. If a firm adopts the green technology, which is environmentally friendly, its marginal cost becomes c_g, where $c_g > c_b$. Additionally, switching to the green technology requires an investment in new equipment, with the investment cost denoted as $K(>0)$.

Assume that both firms produce homogeneous goods, and that their production activities

---

[2] For example, Oliva et al. (2022) conducts an empirical study on adaptation strategies for firms impacted by global warming. In contrast, this study is theoretical and focuses on the adoption of pollution-reducing technologies rather than adaptation strategies. Adaptation measures will be briefly addressed later.

[3] We refer to the setting of Lambertini et al. (2022).

generate negative externalities. These externalities can take various forms, such as greenhouse gas emissions, harmful chemical waste, or noise pollution. The amount of negative externality generated by firm i's production is given by $\theta_j q_i, (\theta \geq 0)$ (where $\theta_b > \theta_g = 0$). This implies that if a firm adopts the green technology ($j = g$), no pollution is generated. Here, q_i represents the production quantity of firm i, so the total pollution generated by both firms, E, is $E = \sum_{i=1}^{2} \theta_j q_i$. The social damage resulting from negative externalities is denoted as $D(E)$ ($D'(E) > 0$).

Firms face a downward-sloping demand curve. In this model, the inverse demand function is given by $p = a - Q, (Q = \sum_{i=1}^{2} q_i)$. It is assumed that consumers in this market do not consider the environmental impact of firms when making their consumption decisions. Also, to ensure an interior solution, we assume $a - 2c_g > 0$.

Next, we assume that the environmental issues caused by the negative externalities generated from the production activities of both firms not only result in social damage but also impact the firms themselves. For example, noise from a neighboring factory might reduce a firm's productivity, or shared natural resources could become polluted due to the actions of both firms, raising the cost of using those resources. Other examples include the negative effects of greenhouse gas emissions, such as rising temperatures or extreme weather events, which could damage production facilities or impair labor productivity.

The extent to which environmental damage caused by a firm or its competitor affects business operations will likely vary depending on the type of environmental issue. Therefore, we introduce a parameter $\alpha(\geq 0)$ to represent the impact of negative externalities caused by the activities of both firms on their production costs. In this model, it is assumed that this effect increases each firm's marginal cost and that the magnitude of the effect grows with the increase in negative externalities. Accordingly, this impact on marginal cost is represented as αE. The key characteristic of this cost impact is that, due to the public good nature of the environment, it affects both firms equally, regardless of which firm is the source of the pollution. In this model, we analyze how firms choose their technology when the negative externalities generated by both their own and their competitor's activities influence their marginal costs.

This model is analyzed as a two-stage game, considering only pure strategies. In the first stage, each firm decides which technology to adopt. Based on the chosen technology, in the second stage, the firms make decisions regarding either the quantity produced or the price.

2.2 Cournot competition

We now analyze the case where Cournot competition takes place in stage 2. The profit of firm i depends on the technology chosen by the rival firm. First, when the rival firm adopts the brown technology, the profit of firm i, assuming it also chooses brown, is given by

$$\pi_i^{bb} = (a - Q - \alpha\theta_b Q)q_i^{bb} \tag{1}$$

In this case, both firms adopt the same technology, and the optimal output is

$$q_i^{bb*} = \frac{a}{3(1+\alpha\theta_b)} \tag{2}$$

Since both firms are using the brown technology, they each generate environmental pollution, with the total pollution being $\theta_b Q$. As a result, the marginal costs of both firms increase due to their own and their rival's actions, with this cost increase represented by $\alpha\theta_b Q(=\alpha E)$ in equation (1). The profit for each firm is

$$\pi_i^{bb*} = \frac{1}{1+\alpha\theta_b}\left(\frac{a}{3}\right)^2 \tag{3}$$

Since $\frac{1}{1+\alpha\theta_b} \leq 1$, it is clear that the cost increase caused by environmental pollution reduces firm profits. Next, consider the case where firm 1 adopts the brown technology and firm 2 adopts the green technology. The profit of firm 1, π_1^{bg}, is given by

$$\pi_1^{bg} = (a - Q - \alpha\theta_b q_1^{bg})q_1^{bg} \tag{4}$$

The profit of firm 2, π_2^{bg}, is given by

$$\pi_2^{bg} = (a - Q - c_g - \alpha\theta_b q_1^{bg})q_2^{bg} - K \tag{5}$$

In this case, both firms' marginal costs increase by $\alpha\theta_b q_1^{bg}$ due to the environmental pollution generated by firm 1. Therefore, in equation (5), firm 2 experiences not only the increased marginal costs from adopting green technology, but also the additional cost increase caused by environmental pollution. In this case, the output of each firm is given by

$$q_1^{bg*} = \frac{a+c_g}{3(1+\alpha\theta_b)}; \quad q_2^{bg*} = \frac{a-2c_g}{3} \tag{6}$$

The corresponding profits for each firm are

$$\pi_1^{bg*} = \frac{1}{1+\alpha\theta_b}\left(\frac{a+c_g}{3}\right)^2; \quad \pi_2^{bg*} = \left(\frac{a-2c_g}{3}\right)^2 - K \tag{7}$$

Next, when both firms adopt the green technology, since $\theta_g = 0$, neither firm generates any negative externalities. The optimal output for each firm in this case is

$$q_i^{gg*} = \frac{a-c_g}{3} \tag{8}$$

The corresponding profit for each firm is

$$\pi_i^{gg*} = \left(\frac{a-c_g}{3}\right)^2 - K \tag{9}$$

Table 1: Cournot competition without environmental regulation

Firm 1 \ Firm 2	green	brown
green	$\left(\frac{a-c_g}{3}\right)^2 - K$, $\left(\frac{a-c_g}{3}\right)^2 - K$	$\left(\frac{a-2c_g}{3}\right)^2 - K$, $\frac{1}{1+\alpha\theta_b}\left(\frac{a+c_g}{3}\right)^2$
brown	$\frac{1}{1+\alpha\theta_b}\left(\frac{a+c_g}{3}\right)^2$, $\left(\frac{a-2c_g}{3}\right)^2 - K$	$\frac{1}{1+\alpha\theta_b}\left(\frac{a}{3}\right)^2$, $\frac{1}{1+\alpha\theta_b}\left(\frac{a}{3}\right)^2$

The left side of each cell shows the profits of Firm 1, while the right side shows those of Firm 2.

Based on the above, the profits of both firms in stage 2 are summarized in a payoff matrix (Table 1). From this, Propositions 1 and 2 can be derived as follows:

Proposition 1

When $\alpha = 0$, neither firm adopts green technology. This result holds even if the investment cost for switching to the green technology, K, is 0.

When $\alpha = 0$, there is no increase in marginal costs due to negative externalities in this model. In this case, the inequality $\left(\frac{a-c_g}{3}\right)^2 - K < \left(\frac{a+c_g}{3}\right)^2$ holds. Therefore, when the rival firm chooses green, it is more profitable for the firm to choose brown.

Next, when the rival firm chooses brown, the inequality $\left(\frac{a-2c_g}{3}\right)^2 - K < \frac{1}{1+\alpha\theta_b}\left(\frac{a}{3}\right)^2$ holds, meaning that choosing brown also yields higher profits for the firm. Thus, the Cournot-Nash equilibrium is for both firms to choose brown.

Proposition 2

When $\alpha > 0$, There exists a situation in which both firms voluntarily choosing green technology is the unique Nash equilibrium.

For $\alpha > 0$, negative externalities can arise from the production activities of both firms. In this case, when the rival firm adopts green technology, the firm will choose to invest in green technology if the following condition is satisfied

$$\left(\frac{a-c_g}{3}\right)^2 - \frac{1}{1+\alpha\theta_b}\left(\frac{a+c_g}{3}\right)^2 \geq K \tag{10}$$

Thus, when $0 < \alpha < \frac{1}{\theta_b}\left\{\left(\frac{a+c_g}{a-c_g}\right)^2 - 1\right\}$, the left-hand side (LHS) of equation (10) becomes negative, and there is no range in which investment $K > 0$ would be made. Therefore, when the rival firm adopts green technology, the firm will choose brown technology. However, when $\frac{1}{\theta_b}\left\{\left(\frac{a+c_g}{a-c_g}\right)^2 - 1\right\} \leq \alpha$, the firm will also choose green technology.

Next, when the rival firm adopts brown technology, the firm will choose to go green if the following condition holds

$$\left(\frac{a-2c_g}{3}\right)^2 - \frac{1}{1+\alpha\theta_b}\left(\frac{a}{3}\right)^2 \geq K \tag{11}$$

Thus, when $0 < \alpha < \frac{1}{\theta_b}\left\{\left(\frac{a}{a-2c_g}\right)^2 - 1\right\}$, the firm will choose brown technology, and when $\frac{1}{\theta_b}\left\{\left(\frac{a}{a-2c_g}\right)^2 - 1\right\} \leq \alpha$, the firm will choose green technology.

From the above, the Cournot-Nash equilibrium in stage 2 is as follows:

- Provided that inequality (11) is satisfied when $\frac{1}{\theta_b}\left\{\left(\frac{a}{a-2c_g}\right)^2 - 1\right\} \leq \alpha$, the equilibrium is {green, green}.
- In the region $\frac{1}{\theta_b}\left\{\left(\frac{a+c_g}{a-c_g}\right)^2 - 1\right\} \leq \alpha$, if inequality (10) is satisfied and inequality (11) is not satisfied, There exist two Nash equilibria: {green, green} and {brown, brown}[4].
- If inequality (10) is not satisfied, the equilibrium is {brown, brown}.

The region where both firms adopting green technology constitutes a Nash equilibrium is indicated by the shaded area in Figure 1[5]. This result indicates that when α is large and the cost of green investment is low, both firms undertake environmentally conscious actions even under voluntary action.

Next, in the decision-making of stage 1, at least when $\frac{1}{\theta_b}\left\{\left(\frac{a}{a-2c_g}\right)^2 - 1\right\} \leq \alpha$ and inequality

---

[4] The inequality $\frac{1}{\theta_b}\left\{\left(\frac{a+c_g}{a-c_g}\right)^2 - 1\right\} < \frac{1}{\theta_b}\left\{\left(\frac{a}{a-2c_g}\right)^2 - 1\right\}$ always holds in this model because it is assumed that $a - 2c_g > 0$.

[5] For the situation where only one firm undertakes green investment does not constitute a Cournot-Nash equilibrium. This is because the intersection of $K = \left(\frac{a-c_g}{3}\right)^2 - \frac{1}{1+\alpha\theta_b}\left(\frac{a+c_g}{3}\right)^2$ and $K = \left(\frac{a-2c_g}{3}\right)^2 - \frac{1}{1+\alpha\theta_b}\left(\frac{a}{3}\right)^2$ does not exist in the region where $K > 0$.

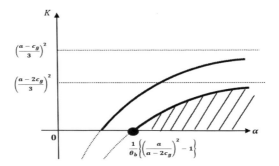

Fig. 1: The region where both firms adopt green technology

(11) is satisfied, it is a subgame perfect equilibrium for both firms to bear the environmental investment cost K.

This represents a situation where green technology is becoming widespread. The following examines the situation where both firms voluntarily undertake green investment within the market mechanism, from the perspective of social welfare.

In an unregulated Cournot market, social welfare in the {brown, brown} scenario is represented as

$$SW^{bb} = 2\pi_i^{bb*} + \frac{1}{2}\left(2q_i^{bb*}\right)^2 - D(\theta_b 2q_i^{bb*}).$$

The first term on the right-hand side (RHS) of the above equation represents the producer surplus and the second term represents the consumer surplus, while the third term denotes the social damage from negative externalities.[6]

On the other hand, social welfare in the {green, green} scenario is represented as

$$SW^{gg} = 2\pi_i^{gg*} + \frac{1}{2}\left(2q_i^{gg*}\right)^2 - 2K.$$

The third term on the RHS of above equation represents the costs associated with green investment. Also, in this case, no negative externalities are generated. Based on the above, the condition under which both firms undertaking green investment is socially desirable is expressed by the following inequality (12).

$$K < 2\pi_i^{gg*} - \left(1 + \frac{1}{1+\alpha\theta_b}\right)\pi_i^{bb*} + \frac{1}{2}D(\theta_b 2q_i^{bb*}) \tag{12}$$

Substituting $\alpha = \frac{1}{\theta_b}\left\{\left(\frac{a}{a-2c_g}\right)^2 - 1\right\}$ into the right-hand side of equation (12) yields a positive value. This indicates that under voluntary initiatives, there is an underinvestment in green

---

[6] SW^{gg} is equal in both regulated and unregulated situations.

technology from the perspective of social welfare. Furthermore, the situation realized in the equilibrium where both firms undertake green investment does not align with the first-best solution. That is, the social welfare in the {green, green} equilibrium is lower than in the first-best state:

$$SW^{fb} = \frac{(a-c_g)^2}{2} - 2K > SW^{gg}$$

While both firms' green investment eliminates negative externalities, the price set in Cournot competition under a duopoly remains higher than the first-best level due to firms' strategic interactions, leading to a welfare loss.

2.3 Bertrand Competition

Next, the case where stage 2 involves Bertrand competition is analyzed. In this model, it is assumed that the two firms produce homogeneous goods, and consumers do not value the firms' efforts to reduce environmental impact. Therefore, if both firms use the same technology, no positive profit can be earned from production. However, when the two firms adopt different technologies, the firm with the lower marginal cost will monopolize the market. Based on this, the payoff matrix for Bertrand competition is summarized in Table 2. In Table 2, $\pi_j^M > 0$ represents the profit of firm i in a monopoly situation[7].

In this case, in stage 2, both firms choosing brown and earning zero profits {brown, brown} constitutes the Bertrand-Nash equilibrium. Therefore, in stage 1, the decision not to invest in pollution-reducing technology becomes the subgame perfect equilibrium. As a result, under Bertrand competition, even if both firms engaging in green investment represents the first-best outcome, this situation cannot be achieved through voluntary action.

3. The Effect of Environmental Policy

Next, the impact of environmental policy on firms' technology choices within this framework is analyzed. In this study, environmental taxes are used as the policy measure. The environmental tax is levied on production that generates negative externalities, with the tax rate t applied per unit of pollution emitted. The tax rate is assumed to be in the range $0 < t < a$. Therefore, firms adopting green technology, which does not generate pollution, are exempt from the tax. In stage 2, under Cournot competition, the profit functions for each firm are as follows:

---

[7] If firm 1 monopolizes the market and its monopoly price is lower than firm 2's marginal cost, it will earn positive profits at the monopoly price. On the other hand, if firm 1's monopoly price is higher than firm 2's marginal cost, firm 1 will set its price slightly below firm 2's marginal cost to earn positive profits. Since determining which of these situations occurs is not the main focus of this analysis, we simply denote this as $\pi_i^M > 0$.

Table 2: Bertrand competition without environmental regulation

Firm 1 \ Firm 2	green	brown
green	$-K, -K$	$-K, \pi_2^M$
brown	$\pi_1^M, -K$	$0, 0$

- When both firms choose brown:
$$\pi_i^{bbt} = (a - Q - t\theta_b - \alpha\theta_b Q)q_i^{bbt}$$
- When firm 1 chooses brown and firm 2 chooses green:
$$\pi_1^{bgt} = (a - Q - t\theta_b - \alpha\theta_b q_1^{bgt})q_1^{bgt}$$
$$\pi_2^{bgt} = (a - Q - c_g - \alpha\theta_b q_1^{bgt})q_2^{bgt} - K$$
- When both firms choose green:
  Since they are not subject to the environmental tax, the profits are the same as in the case without regulation.

Based on these results, the payoff matrix for Cournot competition is summarized in Table 3. When the environmental tax is imposed, the profits for both firms in the case where they adopt green technology remain unchanged from before the tax. However, firms that choose brown technology experience a decrease in profits due to the tax.

Proposition 3

Under Cournot competition, the introduction of an environmental tax increases the incentive for both firms to adopt green technology. However, under Bertrand competition, the situation where both firms adopt green technology does not constitute an equilibrium.

When the rival firm chooses green technology, the condition for the firm to also choose green is given by

$$\left(\frac{a - c_g}{3}\right)^2 - \frac{1}{1 + \alpha\theta_b}\left(\frac{a + c_g - 2t\theta_b}{3}\right)^2 \geq K \qquad (13)$$

This indicates that the range of K in which investment in green technology is broader than in the case without the environmental tax, as shown by equation (10). Furthermore, the range of α required for the LHS of equation (13) to be positive is $\alpha \geq \frac{1}{\theta_b}\left\{\left(\frac{a+c_g-2t}{a-c_g}\right)^2 - 1\right\}$. This shows that the range of α in which green technology is adopted expands to lower values compared to the case without the environmental tax.

Table 3: Cournot competition under environmental regulation

Firm1 \ Firm2	green	brown
green	$\left(\frac{a-c_g}{3}\right)^2 - K$, $\left(\frac{a-c_g}{3}\right)^2 - K$	$\left(\frac{a-2c_g+t\theta_b}{3}\right)^2 - K$, $\frac{1}{1+\alpha\theta_b}\left(\frac{a+c_g-2t\theta_b}{3}\right)^2$
brown	$\frac{1}{1+\alpha\theta_b}\left(\frac{a+c_g-2t\theta_b}{3}\right)^2$, $\left(\frac{a-2c_g+t\theta_b}{3}\right)^2 - K$	$\frac{1}{1+\alpha\theta_b}\left(\frac{a-t\theta_b}{3}\right)^2$, $\frac{1}{1+\alpha\theta_b}\left(\frac{a-t\theta_b}{3}\right)^2$

Next, when the rival firm chooses brown, the condition for the firm to adopt green technology is given by

$$\left(\frac{a-2c_g+t\theta_b}{3}\right)^2 - \frac{1}{1+\alpha\theta_b}\left(\frac{a-t\theta_b}{3}\right)^2 \geq K \tag{14}$$

Compared to the case without the environmental tax (equation (11)), this equation shows an increase in the first term and a decrease in the second term. The increase in the first term reflects the fact that the environmental tax raises the cost of brown technology, making green investment relatively more attractive. At the same time, the decrease in the second term suggests that firms' expected profitability under brown technology declines. This means that firms have a stronger incentive to invest in green technology than before the tax. Additionally, the condition for the LHS of equation (14) to be positive is:

$$\frac{1}{\theta_b}\left\{\left(\frac{a-t\theta_b}{a-2c_g+t\theta_b}\right)^2 - 1\right\} \leq \alpha$$

This indicates that the range of α in which green technology is adopted expands to lower values compared to the case without the tax. In other words, even when α is relatively small, firms are still incentivized to invest in green technology. Consequently, in stage 1, the range where both firms invest in green technology expands. Based on the above, the introduction of an environmental tax in a Cournot market increases the likelihood that both firms adopt green technology and has the potential to enhance social welfare by reducing negative externalities and promoting cleaner production practices.

On the other hand, the impact of introducing an environmental tax under Bertrand competition depends on the level of the tax t, which leads to different outcomes in stage 2. Since the firms produce homogeneous goods, if both adopt brown technology, their post-tax profits remain zero, as they were before the tax. Additionally, if both firms adopt green technology, their profits will be $-K$. When only one firm adopts brown, the equilibrium is determined by the comparison between the marginal cost of the taxed brown firm, $t\theta_b q_b + \alpha\theta_b q_b$, and the marginal cost of the green firm, $c_g + \alpha\theta_b q_b$.

If the rival firm adopts green technology and the brown firm's production is very small, the condition $t\theta_b q_b < c_g$ holds, allowing the brown firm to still earn positive profits. Therefore, when the rival firm chooses green, the brown firm will choose to remain brown. In this case, if the tax rate is low, the brown firm will dominate the market, and the green firm's profit will be $-K$. However, if the tax rate is high, the brown firm's marginal cost will exceed the green firm's marginal cost within the range where demand exists, enabling the green firm to produce and earn profits greater than $-K$. However, if the tax rate is high, the brown firm's marginal cost will exceed the green firm's marginal cost within the range where demand exists, enabling the green firm to produce and earn profits greater than $-K$. Next, when the rival firm adopts brown, if the environmental tax is low, the firm will also choose brown and earn zero profit. If the tax rate is high, the firm will choose green. Thus, in stage 2 of Bertrand competition, the Nash equilibrium is {brown, brown} when the environmental tax is low, and {green, brown} or {brown, green} when the tax is high.

As a result, there is no situation where both firms adopt green technology. Therefore, the effect of environmental policy under Bertrand competition on the adoption of green technology is limited. In the absence of the policy, the Nash equilibrium would be for both firms to choose brown. However, with a high tax rate, a situation may arise where only one firm chooses green. While an equilibrium where only one firm adopts green under Bertrand competition may occur, this could still be effective from the perspective of reducing negative externalities. When a high environmental tax is imposed, the brown firm's production becomes very small. This is because, with a high tax rate, the brown firm's marginal cost exceeds the green firm's marginal cost even at low production levels. Thus, the introduction of a high environmental tax reduces the brown firm's production, thereby reducing the negative externalities $\alpha \theta_b q_b$.

4. Discussion

When stage 2 is a Cournot market, the existence of a Nash equilibrium in which both firms adopt green technology has been demonstrated. Here, we explore how the option for firms to implement adaptive responses in this analytical framework might affect the adoption and dissemination of green technology. In other words, this framework introduces a scenario in which, in addition to the option of controlling negative externalities by adopting green technologies, firms can also lessen the impact of these externalities on themselves through adaptive measures.

If firms can implement adaptive measures to offset increases in their marginal costs due to negative externalities, they may choose adaptive responses over green technology. For instance, in stage 1 of the game, a firm might choose among (i) investing in green technology to reduce negative externalities, (ii) not investing, or (iii) investing in facilities to counter the marginal cost increase caused by negative externalities. Selecting (i) could still result in increased marginal costs if the competing firm generates negative externalities. Conversely, by choosing (iii), a firm could generate negative externalities itself while controlling the associated marginal cost increase. Thus, the option to implement adaptive measures could have a negative impact on the adoption and spread of green technology.

5. Concluding Remarks

This study analyzed technology choices in a duopoly market under conditions where the occurrence of negative externalities not only causes harm to external parties but also increases the marginal costs of the firms responsible for these externalities. The analysis revealed that under Cournot competition, when this effect is absent, neither firm adopts environmentally friendly technology through voluntary approaches. However, when the effect is present, both firms have an incentive to adopt green technology even in a situation where consumers do not consider environmental concerns. On the other hand, in Bertrand competition, even with this effect, neither firm chooses to adopt green technology.

Furthermore, the introduction of an environmental tax was shown to increase the likelihood of both firms adopting green technology in Cournot competition, whereas in Bertrand competition, the effect of the tax is limited, and only one firm is likely to adopt green technology.

For future research, it would be beneficial to include situations where firms can choose not only mitigation strategies but also adaptation strategies when negative externalities impact the firms responsible for them. Additionally, while this study assumed that the damage caused by negative externalities equally affects both firms, incorporating asymmetric impacts could enable a more comprehensive analysis of diverse environmental issues and technology choices.

References

[1] Amacher, G. S., Koskela, E. and M. Ollikainen (2004) "Environmental quality competition and eco-labeling," *Journal of Environmental Economics and Management*, vol. 47, pp. 284–306.

[2] Arora, S. and S. Gangopadhyay (1995) "Toward a theoretical model of voluntary overcompliance," *Journal of Economic Behavior and Organization*, vol. 28, pp. 289-309.

[3] Buccella, D., L. Fanti and L. Gori (2021) "To abate, or not to abate? A strategic approach on green production in Cournot and Bertrand duopolies," *Energy Economics*, vol. 96, pp.1-15.

[4] Conrad, K. (2005) "Price competition and product differentiation when consumers care for the environment," *Environmental and Resource Economics,* vol31, pp.1-19.

[5] Innes, R. and J. J. Bial (2002) "Inducing innovation in the environmental technology of oligopoly firms," *Journal of Industrial Economics*, 50(3), pp. 265～287.

[6] Khanna, M. (2001) "Non-mandatory approaches to environmental protection," *Journal of Economic Surveys*, vol.15 (3), pp. 291-324.

[7] Lambertini, L., Pignataro, G. and A. Tampieri (2022) "Competition among coalitions in a cournot industry: a validation of the porter hypothesis," *The Japanese Economic Review*, vol. 73, pp 679-713.

[8] Lambertini, L., Poyago-Theotoky, J., A. Tampieri, (2017) "Cournot competition and green innovation: An inverted-U relationship," *Energy Economics*, vol. 68, pp. 116–123.

[9] Linnenluecke, M. K., Stathakis, A., A. Griffiths, (2011) "Firm relocation as adaptive response to climate change and weather extremes," *Global Environmental Change*, vol. 21, pp.123-133.

[10] Milliman, S.R., Prince, R. (1989) "Firm incentives to promote technological change in pollution control," *Journal of Environmental Economics and Management*, vol. 17 (3), pp. 247–265.

[11] Montero, J. P. (2002a) "Permits, standards, and technology innovation," *Journal of Environmental Economics and Management*, vol. 44 (1), pp. 23–44.

[12] Montero, J. P. (2002b) "Market structure and environmental innovation," *Journal of Applied Economics*, vol. 5 (2), pp. 293–325.

[13] Oliva, R. D. P., Huaman, J., Vasquez-Lavin, F., M. Barrientos, (2022) "Firms adaptation to climate change through product innovation," *Journal of Cleaner Production*, vol. 350, 131436.

[14] Segerson, K. (2013) "Voluntary approaches to environmental protection and resource management," *Annual Review of Resource Economics,* vol. 5, pp.161-80.

[15] Segerson, K. and T. J. Miceli (1998) "Voluntary environmental agreements: Good or bad news for environmental protection?," *Journal of Environmental Economics and Management*, vol. 36, pp 109-130.

Chapter 3

Dynamics and Growth Policies of Japanese Economy

Shohei Katayama
Faculty of Economic Sciences, Hiroshima Shudo University
1-1-1, Ozuka-higashi, Asaminami-ku, Hiroshima, 731-3195, JAPAN

Abstract

Japanese economy has encountered secular stagnation for thirty years. The growth rate, the rate of inflation and the interest rate remain low. And the population is decreasing. The performance of Japanese economy has greatly changed at the beginning of 1990s.

Hansen argued the secular stagnation in 1930s. And Summers, Gordon , Acemoglu and Aghion et.al. revived the secular stagnation after the world financial crisis. The secular stagnation was argued from demand side and supply side. Japan has encountered the secular stagnation for thirty years and so we mainly consider it by using growth models.

We develop three growth models and in particular Scumpeterian model in which growth is generated by a random sequence of quality-improving innovations. In the context of a Scumpeterian model with capital accumulation, the capital stock and the innovation rate are jointly determined and influence each other. And so we think that the model can bring the rich and effective growth policies for Japan. We will mention the effects of decrease in population on economy.

Key Words:
Innovation, Endogenous Growth, Decline in Population, Secular Stagnation

1. Introduction

After second world war Japan had recovered for about ten years. Then Japanese economy had made rapid growth until the beginning of 1970s and after that it had made steady growth until the beginning of 1990s. At the beginning of 1990s. the explosion of bubble attacked Japan. Japanese economy has made slow growth since then.

Japanese economy has nearly stopped progress for thirty years. Some of people call this secular stagnation. The growth rate, the rate of inflation, and the interest rate have been low. And the population is decreasing, and decreasing birthrates and an aging population are going on. The performance of Japanese economy has greatly changed at the beginning of 1990s.

Hansen argued the secular stagnation at the end of 1930s. And Summers, Gordon , Acemoglu and Aghion et.al. revived the secular stagnation after the world financial crisis. The secular stagnation was argued from demand side and supply side. Some economists say that Japan has encountered the secular stagnation for thirty years and so we mainly consider it from supply side.

We develop three representative growth models and in particular focus on a growth model, in which growth is generated by a random sequence of quality-improving innovations. It is called Schumpeterian model because it embodies the force that Scumpeter called "creative destruction."

In the context of a Scumpeterian model with capital accumulation, the capital stock and the innovation rate are jointly determined and influence each other. And so it can bring the rich and effective growth policies for Japan with decreasing population. After we inspect the facts of Japanese economy and present basic growth models, we summarize the policies for growth based on that. And we will mention the effects of decline in population on the process of economic growth.

2. Facts of Japanese Economy

2.1 GDP

There are two features in recent Japanese economy. The first one is the low rate of economic growth. The second one is the decrease in population, declining birthrates and an aging population. And the low rate of economic growth has brought about with the decreasing population. It seems that the two are closely related with each other.

Real GDP and Real GDP per capita are considered as the most important macroeconomic variables in economic growth. We look at their movements over time. The real GDP had increased quickly at about 10% for 1956-1973 and had increased steadily at about 5% for 1974-1990. Since 1990 the growth rate of real GDP has repeated to increase or decrease around about 1%. In some years the growth rate was minus.

The real GDP per capita had increased largely until 1991. But it has increased not so much since 1991. The growth rate of real GDP was high in 1960s. But the growth rate of real GDP per capita has been decreasing over time and remains low level at about 1% in recent years.

The rate of economic growth in Japan has been decreasing since the 1990s and that was caused mainly by the drops of contribution in total factor productivity and capital stock. The decline in labor input brought about the decrease in economic growth rate directly. And the decline brought about the decrease in economic growth rate by causing lowering of contribution in total factor productivity and

Figure 1. Growth rate of real GDP in Japan, 1960-2023

capital stock indirectly.

There are three supply factors which yields real GDP. They are labor, capital stock, and total factor productivity. The Increase in capital stock and total factor productivity contributed much to the development of Japanese economy. But the increase in labor contributed not so much to the development of Japanese economy.

The rate of economic growth in Japan has been decreasing since the 1990s and that was caused mainly by the drops of contribution in total factor productivity and capital stock. The decline in labor input brought about the decrease in economic growth rate directly. And the decline brought about the decrease in economic growth rate by causing lowering of contribution in total factor productivity and capital stock indirectly.

Figure 2. Growth rate of real GDP per capita in Japan, 1960-2023.

There are four demand factors which yields real GDP. They are consumption, investment, public expenditure and net export. The Increase in consumption and investment contributed much to the development of Japanese economy. The increase in public expenditure and net export contributed not so much to the development of Japanese economy.

The rate of economic growth in Japan has been decreasing since 1990s and that was caused mainly by the drop of consumption and investment. The contribution to economic growth through public expenditure has been declining since 2013. The contribution to economic growth by net export has been little and constant over time. After all the growth rates of consumption and investment have been much decreasing respectively and that has contributed to the drop of GDP growth rate with the decline in population in Japan.

2.2 Population

Japanese population has been decreasing for more than ten years. And the share of young people has been decreasing and the share of old people has been increasing recently in Japan. Japan had the peak of population in 2008 and then the increase in population turned to the decrease in population.

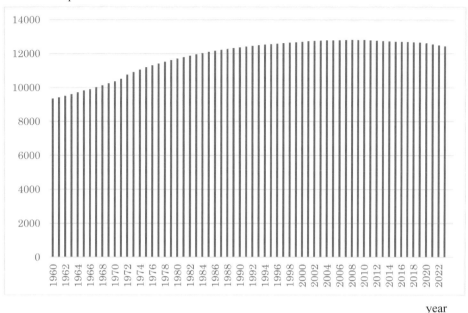

Figure 3. Population in Japan, 1960-2023

The change of population and the change rate of population in Japan tend to move the same direction. Since the latter half of 1990s these have tended to decrease. The average in population decrease was more than five hundred thousand persons and the average rate in population decrease was more than 0.5% for the period 2019-2022.

The working-age population which belongs to 15-64 years had the peak of it in 1995. Since the year it has been decreasing and in 2020 it had the decrease by about fourteen% from the peak. The working-age population which was about eighty-seven million persons in 1995 declined to about seventy-five million persons in 2020.

The birth rate is the number of babies born per thousand persons and the rate in Japan is less than the rate in other advanced countries at present. The number of babies born has been decreasing since 2011 and the number in 2022 was less than eight hundred thousand. It was about seven hundred and thirty thousand in 2023.

The total fertility rate tends to decrease and becomes about 1.2 in 2023. This brings the decrease in number of babies born. The number of deaths has been increasing and was over the number of births fifteen years ago. As a result, the population in Japan has been decreasing for fifteen years.

2.3 Secular Stagnation

There were two famous economists who argued about population and economy. The one is Malthus, who published An Essay on the Principle of Population in 1798. He was anxious about over population. For the main industry in his age was agriculture in which production was limited. The other cone is Keynes, who lectured on Some Economic Consequences of Declining Population in 1937. He argued that the declining population would causes the decreases in consumption and investment and the decreases would cause the decreases in production and income. As a result, there are a possibility that the economy will fall into a serious stagnation in the future.

The great depression attacked US and the other countries in 1930s. Observing the depression, Hansen advocated the theory of secular stagnation at the American Economic Association in 1938. He argued that as the capitalism made progress, the rate of economic growth declined. Decreases in inventions or population reduce the investment opportunity, which brings the secular stagnation and the decline in potential growth rate (Hansen (1939)).

After world financial crisis Summers advocated the theory of secular stagnation again at the IMF meeting in 2013. The theory of Summers(2014),(2015) is like the one of Hansen and regarded the over saving, the insufficiency of investment, and the decrease in population as important causes of secular stagnation. He showed that the decline in labor population and the fall in investment led to the secular stagnation. That is, the fall in investment and aggregate demand with the decrease in population brings the decrease in potential growth rate and the secular stagnation ("hysteresis effect").

Gordon focused on the population and the technology. He argued the theory mainly from supply side and in his opinion as economy make progress, great inventions decline. He showed that TFP (from 1970s) remained one-third of TFP (1920-1970) in US. That brought the decrease in opportunity of investment and the decline in potential growth rate, together with the decrease in population. After all he described that the remarkable economic growth (1870-1970) was an exception and the rate of economic growth and the rate of increase in consumption would reduce by half in the future (Gordon(2012),(2016)).

The effects of decline in labor population to economic growth depend on that new technology is complement to or substitute for labor. As the new technology is compliment to labor, the decline in labor population will decrease the productivity of capital and technology and hold back the capital accumulation and technology progress. On the other hand, as the new technology is substitute for labor, the decline in labor population will increase the productivity of capital and technology by introducing robot and AI. That can promote the capital accumulation and the technology progress and bring about the increase in output (Accemoglu etc.(2016), (2017),(2018)).

3. Representative Models

3.1 The neoclassical growth model

The origin of neoclassical growth model is Solow (1956). In this section we develop basic Solow model. The Solow model is built around a production function and a capital accumulation equation.

Output, Y is produced by combing physical capital, K and labor, L. The production function (1) exhibits constant returns to scale tacitly.

$$Y = F(K, AL) \tag{1}$$

where A represents labor-augmenting technology that grows exogenously at rate g. We assume that there is no difference between the labor and the population and they growth at a constant rate n.

Physical capital is accumulated by investing some output instead of consuming it as

$$\dot{K} = \frac{dK}{dt} = sY - \delta K \tag{2}$$

where s is a constant saving rate (= a constant investment rate for physical capital) and δ is a fixed rate of capital depreciation.

First, we let lowercase letters denote variables divided by the effective labor, AL, and rewrite the production function in terms of output per effective labor as

$$\tilde{y} = f(\tilde{k})$$

where $\tilde{y}$ is the output per effective labor, and $\tilde{k}$ is the capital stock per effective labor.

The capital accumulation equation can be written in terms of the state variables as

$$\dot{\tilde{k}} = sf(\tilde{k}) - (\delta + g + n)\tilde{k} \tag{3}$$

where n is exogenous growth rate of labor and g is exogenous growth rate of technology. From equation (3), the steady-state capital stock per effective labor, $\tilde{k}$ is given, using equation (4),

$$sf(\tilde{k}) = (\delta + g + n)\tilde{k} . \tag{4}$$

Along the balanced growth $\tilde{y}$ and $\tilde{k}$ are constant, equations (5) and (6) are brought.

$$\dot{Y}/Y = \dot{K}/K = g + n \tag{5}$$

$$\dot{y}/y = \dot{Y}/Y - n = \dot{k}/k = \dot{K}/K - n = g \tag{6}$$

where y is output per capita, and k is capital stock per labor. Along the balanced growth both the growth rate in output or the capital stock are the sum of labor growth rate and technology growth rate. And both growth rate in output per labor and capital stock per labor depend on only exogenous technology growth rate and nothing except technology growth rate affects the growth rate in output per capita and the growth rate in capital stock per labor in the long run.

3.2 The Romer model

The Romer model endogenizes technological progress by introducing the search for new ideas by researchers. As a result, output per capita and capital stock per labor continue to grow at a constant rate. We will look at the basic structure of the Romer model. For simplification, we assume the followings. The basic Romer model does not include the intermediate goods which original Romer model includes explicitly and the ratio of labor for research to labor for output is a constant, given exogenously.

The aggregate production function in the Romer model describes how the capital stock and effective labor produce output :

$$Y = F(K, AL_Y) \tag{7}$$

where the output has a constant return in the two inputs.

The accumulation equations for capital and labor are identical to those for the neoclassical model. Capital accumulates as people in the economy save or invest at a given rate, s from their income and the capital stock depreciates at a exogenous rate δ:

$$\dot{K} = sY - \delta K. \tag{8}$$

Labor, which is equivalent to the population, is fixed or grows exponentially at some constant and exogenous rate n:

$$\frac{\dot{L}}{L} = n$$

According to the Romer model, $A(t)$ is the stock of knowledge or the number of ideas that have been invented until time t. In the basic version of the model, $\dot{A}$ is equal to the number of people attempting to discover new ideas, L_A, multiplied by the rate at which they discover new ideas, $\bar{z}$:

$$\dot{A} = \bar{z} L_A. \tag{9}$$

We suppose that the productivity of researcher $\bar{z}$ is proportional to the stock of ideas:

$$\bar{z} = zA \tag{10}$$

where z shows a fixed number.

Equation (9) and (10) together lead to equation (11):

$$\dot{A} = zL_A A \tag{11}$$

All of the labor in the economy L is allocated the labor to produce output L_Y and the labor to produce ideas L_A:

$$L_Y + L_A = L.$$

We assume that a constant fraction, $L_A/L = l$ of the labor force engages in R&D to produce new ideas, and the remaining fraction, $1 - l$, produces output.

Using this with equation (11) yields

$$\dot{A}/A = zL_A = zlL \qquad (12)$$

$\dot{A}/A$ is constant over time.

Along a balanced growth path, as L is constant (with $n = o$), a constant $Y/(AL_Y)$, $K/(AL_Y)$ lead to

$$\dot{Y}/Y = \dot{K}/K = zlL. \qquad (13)$$

And so the growth rate g in this model depends on the productivity in research z, the fraction of researcher l, and the population L. They are greater, the rate of growth is higher. The saving rate doesn't affect the growth rate in the long run, that is, the rise in saving rate doesn't increase the growth rate in the long run.

Considering duplication and fishing effects, Jones (1995), (2013) suggested the following general production function for ideas:

$$\dot{A} = zL_A^\lambda A^\phi \qquad 0 < \lambda < 1, \ 0 < \phi < 1 \qquad (14)$$

Dividing both sides of equation (14) by A, yields

$$\dot{A}/A = zL_A^\lambda / A^{1-\phi}. \qquad (15)$$

Along a balanced growth path, $\dot{A}/A (= zL_A^\lambda/A^{1-\varphi})$ is constant. And using this with $\dot{L}_A/L_A = n$ yields

$$\dot{A}/A = \frac{\lambda}{1-\phi} n. \qquad (16)$$

This implies that the growth rate for ideas is directly proportional to the growth rate of the population n.

Letting g_x denote the growth rate of some variable x along the balanced growth path, we see easily that

$$g_y = g_k = g_A.$$

Rewriting this by aggregate terms yields

$$\dot{Y}/Y = \dot{K}/K = \frac{\lambda + 1 - \phi}{1 - \phi} n. \qquad (17)$$

After all the growth rate of output and capital stock are directly proportional to the growth rate of the population respectively.

3.3 The Schumpeterian Model

Innovation-based growth models consist of two parallel branches. The One branch is the product-variety model of Romer (1990), but in which innovation causes productivity growth by creating new, but not necessarily improved, varieties of product. Romer model viewed technological progress as an increase in the number of intermediate goods and this increase brings the increase of productivity. Once invented, each variety of intermediate good continues to used forever.

The other one is the quality improvements model and was developed in Aghion and Howitt (1992), (1998), (2009) and Grossman and Helpman (1991). This type of growth theory allows for an innovation to replace an existing intermediate good in the production process.

Schumpeter discussed capitalism as a process of creative destruction, in which existing businesses and technologies were replaced by new ones. The continual obsolescence of old techniques appears as new ones are invented, improving the productivity of the economy at each step.

That is, Schumpeterian growth theory focuses on quality-improving innovation where new product render old products obsolete and hence involves the force called creative destruction. We present a basic Schumpeterian model (Aghion and Howitt (2009)) and consider the process of growth according to the model.

(Model)

There is a constant population and each person is endowed with one unit of skilled labor. People consume the final good, which is produced by perfectly competitive firms. The final good is produced under perfect competition according to the product function:

$$Y_t = A_t^{1-\alpha} L_t^{1-\alpha} x_t^\alpha, \qquad 0 < \alpha < 1 \qquad (18)$$

where Y_t is the output of final good in period t, and A_t is a parameter which reflects the productivity of intermediate good in that period, and A_t term captures the latest available technology. x_t is the amount of intermediate good used in that period and L_t is the labor supply used for final good production.

Intermediate good is produced according to the production function:

$$x_t = K_t$$

where K_t is the amount of capital used as input. So the monopolist's cost is now $R_{kt} K_t = R_{kt} x_t$ where R_{kt} is the rental price of capital in period t. The monopolist in intermediate good uses the demand curve in final good (price=marginal productivity) and has the following equation:

$$p_t = \alpha A_t^{1-\alpha} x_t^{\alpha-1} L_t^{1-\alpha}$$

where p_t is the price of intermediate good relative to the final good. By using this we have the monopolist' profit:

$$\pi_t = \alpha A_t^{1-\alpha} x_t^{\alpha} L_t^{1-\alpha} - R_{kt} x_t, \qquad (19)$$

and maximizing the profit brings the quantity of intermediate good:

$$x_t = (\alpha^2 / R_{kt})^{\frac{1}{1-\alpha}} A_t L_t. \qquad (20)$$

Equation (20) follows from the first-order condition for optimization.

Using (20), we can write the equilibrium condition of capital market as

$$K_t = (\alpha^2 / R_{kt})^{\frac{1}{1-\alpha}} A_t L_t. \qquad (21)$$

In this paragraph we denote the aggregate capital stock per effective labor as

$$k_t = K_t / A_t L_t.$$

This and equation (21) lead to

$$R_{kt} = \alpha^2 k_t^{\alpha-1}. \qquad (22)$$

By using equations (20)-(22) and the definition of k_t, we have the equilibrium amount of intermediate good:

$$x_t = A_t (K_t / A_t) = A_t L_t k_t. \qquad (23)$$

Substituting from equations (22) and (23) into equation ((29), we see that

$$\pi_t = \tilde{\pi}(k_t) A_t L_t \qquad (24)$$

where the productivity-adjusted profit function

$$\tilde{\pi}(k_t) = \alpha(1-\alpha) k_t^{\alpha}$$

is increasing in the capital stock per effective labor k_t, because an increase in k_t reduces the monopolist's unit cost of production, which is R_{kt}.

Using equation (23) to substitute for x_t, we can rewrite equation (18) as

$$Y_t = A_t L_t k_t^{\alpha} \qquad (25)$$

Which is the production function used in the neoclassical model. In particular, the productivity parameter A_t is the index of labor-augmenting productivity.

(Innovation and Capital Accumulation)

An entrepreneur tries to innovate in every period. If she succeeds, she will become the (next period) monopolist, with a productivity parameter $A_t = \gamma A_{t-1}$, where $\gamma > 1$. The probability of her success will be $\mu_t \in (0,1) = \varphi(r_t) = \lambda r_t^{\sigma}$ where $r_t = R_t / A_t^* L_t$ and $A_t^* = \gamma A_t$, the target productivity level. We assume λ and σ small enough that $\mu < 1$.

Her research expenditure R_t is determined to maximize her net expected benefit:

$$\varphi(R_t / A_t^* L_t) \pi_t^* - R_t$$

where π_t^* is her profit brought by success. The first order condition for maximization is

$$\varphi'(R_t/A_t^*L)\pi_t^*/A_t^*L_t - 1 = 0.$$

Rewriting it by using equation (24) gives the optimal research equation,

$$\varphi'(r_t)\tilde{\pi}(k_t) = 1 \qquad (R)$$

Since an increase in k_t raises the monopoly profit that constitutes the reward for innovation, the productivity-adjusted level of research r_t is an increasing function of the capital stock per effective worker k_t. And the productivity growth rate g_t is the frequency of innovations $\varphi(r_t)$ times the size $(\gamma - 1)$.

$$g_t = \varphi(r_t) \times (\gamma - 1)$$

We can solve equation (R) for $r_t = [\sigma\lambda\tilde{\pi}(k_t)]^{\frac{1}{1-\sigma}}$ and $\mu_t = \lambda[\sigma\lambda\tilde{\pi}(k_t)]^{\frac{\sigma}{1-\sigma}}$, so we have $\tilde{g}(k_t) = (\gamma - 1)\lambda[\sigma\lambda\tilde{\pi}(k_t)]^{\frac{\sigma}{1-\sigma}}$. After all the productivity growth is also an increasing function in the capital stock per effective worker.

$$g_t = \tilde{g}(k_t), \quad \tilde{g}' > 0$$

As in neoclassical model, we have the equation (26) that describes capital accumulation or growth with a fixed saving rate s and a fixed depreciation rate δ.

$$\dot{K}_t = sY_t - \delta K_t = sA_t^{1-\alpha}K_t^\alpha L_t^{1-\alpha} - \delta K_t \qquad (26)$$

It states that net increase in capital stock equals gross investment sY_t minus depreciation δK_t.

Dividing equation (26) by K_t gives equation (27).

$$\dot{K}_t/K_t = (sY_t - \delta K_t)/K_t = sA^{1-\alpha}K^{\alpha-1}L_t^{1-\alpha} - \delta \qquad (27)$$

(Steady-State)

The steady-state values g and k of growth rate g_t and capital-stock per effective worker k_t are define respectively

$$g = \tilde{g}(k) \qquad (28)$$

and

$$sk^{\alpha-1} = g + \delta + n. \qquad (29)$$

The last equation is identical to the condition defining the steady-state capital stock per effective labor. In steady state k_t is constant and the growth rate of capital stock must equal the growth rate of effective labor. The two equations (28) and (29) are represented, by the curves RR and KK in Figure 4, respectively. An increase in the capital stock per effective labor raises the incentive to innovate and hence spurs productivity growth. And so the research equation RR is upward sloping. The capital stock per effective worker is a decreasing function of the growth rate according to equation (29). And so the capital curve KK is downward sloping.

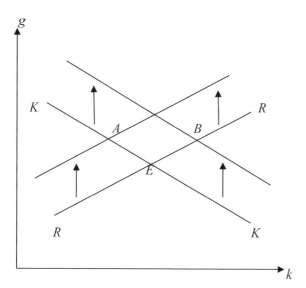

Figure 4. Steady State

Changes in the size of innovations γ or the efficiency of research λ disturb the research equation (28) and will shift the RR curve, causing k and g to move in the opposite direction. And an increase in the size of innovations γ or the efficiency of research λ will shift RR curve up. That is, this shift will raise long-run growth, and reduce the long-run capital stock per effective worker in the steady state.

On the other hand changes in saving rate s or depreciation rate δ disturb capital equation (29) and will shift the KK curve, causing k and g to move in the same direction. Thus an increase in the saving rate s or a decrease in the depreciation rate δ will raise not only the long-run stock of capital per labor, but also the long-run growth rate because the rise in k will strengthen the incentive to do the research and enhances the productivity.

In the long run the economy's growth rate will equal the rate of labor-augmenting technological progress. But this equality does not mean that only technological progress causes economic growth, because g is now endogenous. In this model the long-run growth rate will be influenced not only by the research equation that governs innovation, but also by the capital accumulation equation.

For example, when the increase in incentives to perform R&D will result in a higher g, we regard the increase as a source of economic growth, since it was brought by leftward shift in RR curve on Figure 4. But the increase in saving rate s will displace the KK curve on Figure 4 to the right, again causing g to go up. In this case we regard the increase in s as a source of economic growth.

In one case the economic growth is caused by innovation with $n = 0$ and in other case it is caused by capital accumulation. And so we can argue a causal relationship for growth in the context of a Schumpeterian model, where the capital stock and the innovation rate are jointly determined and influence each other.

4. Policies for Growth

According to the fact and model as described, we consider the policy for economic growth. In Japan the rate of growth has dropped since 1990s and the working-age population has been declining since the year 1995. From demand side the consumption and the investment have contributed to the growth rate of GDP less and from supply side TFP and capital stock have contributed to the growth rate of GDP less since the year 1991.

The indexes of unemployment rate, inflation rate, interest rate, and GDP gap have remained at low level for last thirty years. And so we regard supply side as more important cause for last thirties' stagnation and explore the policies for growth theoretically and positively.

In neoclassical growth model the growth rate of real GDP per capita depends on only the exogenous rate of technological progress along the balanced growth. Only the rise in exogenous rate of technological progress goes up the growth rate of real GDP per capita. However, because this implies that the rate of technological progress, the growth rate of real GDP per capita is black box, we can't argue about growth policy in neoclassical growth model.

In basic Romer model the growth rate of real GDP per capita is equal to the growth rate of ideas along the balanced growth. This determinant looks like that of the growth rate in neoclassical growth model. The growth rate of real GDP per capita, the growth rate of ideas follows from the of productivity of research z, ratio of researcher l, and population L. That is, the growth rate of ideas is determined endogenously by the productivity of research, ratio of researcher and population.

The rises in the productivity of research z, the ratio of researcher l, or the population L go up the growth rate of real GDP per capita along the balanced growth. Because we can't expect the increase in population at present, we need to engage in the rise in productivity of research and ratio of researcher as growth policy. The investment for education and training will contribute to the rise in productivity of research and ratio of researcher.

According to Romer model the population expansion goes up the rate of economic growth ("size effect") but we couldn't expect that in Japan where the population has been decreasing. Incidentally in the original Romer model the innovation is the increase in number of intermediate goods and it promote the economic growth.

In Schumpeterian model the research equation (28) and the capital accumulation equation (29) determine the g and the k along balanced growth. And the capital accumulation as well as the research progress the economic growth. The shift of equation (28), RR curve or equation (29), KK curve change g and k along balanced growth.

RR curve is upward sloping and KK curve is downward sloping. The rise in size of innovation γ or productivity of research λ brings upward shifts of RR curve. That brings the reduction in k and the rise in g and they move in the opposite direction from their destination. Therefore we regard the rise in size of innovation γ or productivity of research λ as important causes for economic growth. As firm's R&D is subsidized by government, the growth rate will be go up through spurring R&D. Further, to spur R&D and rearise the creative destruction, more fierce competitions and the promotion of start-up will be needed. As Aghion et.al state, big companies which are in safe position will not have so much incentives to develop new technologies.

The rise in saving rate s or the decline in capital depreciation δ brings the upward shift of KK curve. That brings the rise in k and g and they move the same direction from their destination. After all we regard the rise in saving rate s or the decline in capital depreciation δ as important causes for economic growth too. This unique result is yielded by basic Schumpeterian model but isn't yielded by neoclassical growth model and basic Romer model.

Next, we consider the effect of change in population on economic growth. As we review the equation (29), we suppose that the decline in growth rate of population n brings about the rise in capital stock k_t through the rise in capital equipment per capita. The decline in n brings the rise in k and reduces the rental price of capital stock, which increases the profit. Then KK curve shifts rightward and brings the rise in k and g along balanced growth. In this case the size effect of population growth towards the same direction might be accepted.

In Aghion et al. (2016) carbon taxes are regarded as effective and recommended to combat climate change. In their model consumers derive utility from an outside good and from motor vehicle services. And they show that firms tend to innovate more in clean technology when they face higher tax-inclusive fuel prices in the automobile industry. Furthermore, there is path dependence in type of innovation (clean/dirty) both from aggregate spillovers and from the firm's own innovation history. They simulate the increases in carbon taxes needed to allow clean technologies to overtake dirty technologies.

In Acemoglu et al. (2016) an endogenous growth model is developed. A representative household derives utility from life time consumption. And Research can be directed to either technology. If dirty technology is more advanced, the transition to clean technology can be difficult. Carbon taxes and research subsidies may encourage the production and the innovation in clean technologies, though the transition will typically slow. They estimate the model, using microdata from US energy sector. They then characterize the optimal policy path that heavily relies on both subsidies and taxes. Relying only on carbon taxes or delaying intervention have significant welfare costs.

5. Conclusion

Since 1955 Japanese economy had made rapid growth until the beginning of 1970s and then it had made steady growth until the beginning of 1990s. Since beginning of 1990s. the Japanese economy has made slow growth. As a result, the growth rate of real GDP per capita has increased slowly.

Japanese economy has stopped progress for thirty years. Some of people call this secular stagnation. The growth rate, the rate of inflation, and the interest rate have been low. And the population is decreasing, and the declining birth rate and the aging population is going on in recent Japan. After all the performance of Japanese economy has greatly changed in 1990s.

Hansen argued the secular stagnation in the end of 1930s. And Summers and Gordon argued it from demand side and supply side respectively. Some economists say that Japan has encountered the secular stagnation for thirty years or more, and therefore we mainly considered it by using growth theory.

We developed three representative growth models, a neoclassical model and two models based on R&D. In particular we focus on Scumpeterian model in which growth is endogenously generated by a random sequence of quality-improving innovation.

In the context of basic Scumpeterian model with capital accumulation, the capital stock and the innovation rate are jointly determined and influence each other. And so it can bring more rich and effective growth policies for Japan with decreasing population.

The increases in size of innovations or efficiency of research are recommended as growth policy according to growth theory based on R&D. R&D should be subsidized or reduced taxes by the government to increase the size of innovations or the efficiency of research. Rise in saving rate increases the capital stock and lead to innovation. Investment in education and training will promote R&D and innovation. And the competition between firms by innovation will promote growth.

In basic Romer model the decrease in population leads to the decrease in growth rate of ideas. However, the decline in growth rate of population may not reduce R$D and innovation. For in basic Schmpeterian model there is a possibility that the decline increases real GDP per capita and R&D through the rise in capital equipment per capita.

Further the decline in population will improve environment and keep exhaustible resources for a long time through the repression in aggregate production and consumption. Large subsidies to clean technology or high fuel taxes will promote clean technology and block that the environment becomes worse.

Finally, we would like to point out the limitation of this study. This study does not discuss Japanese secular stagnation under open economy. This issue need to be addressed in future studies.

References

[1] Acemoglu, D. and P. Restrepo (2017). "Secular Stagnation? The effect aging on Economic Growth in the age of Automation," *A.E.R.*107(5) : 174-179.

[2] Acemoglu, D. and P. Restrepo (2018), "The Race between Man and Machine: Implication of Technology for Growth, Factor Shares, and Employment," *A.E.R.* 108(6):1488-1542.

[3] Acemoglu, D., U. Akcigit, D. Hanley, W. Kerr (2016), "Transition to Technology," *J.P.E.*124(1):52-104.

[4] Aghion, P., and P. Howitt. (1992)."A Model of Growth through Creative Destruction."*Econometrica*,60:323-351.

[5] Aghion, P., and P. Howitt. (1998). *Endogenous Growth Theory*. Cambridge, MA: MIT Press.

[6] Aghion, P. and P. Howitt. (2009). *The Economics of Growth*. Cambridge, MA: MIT Press.

[7] Aghion, P., D. A. Dechezlepretre, D. Hemous, R. Martin, and J. V. Reenen (2016)," Carbon Taxes, Path dependency, and Directed Technical Change : Evidence from the Auto Industry," *J.P.E.*124(1):1-51.

[8] Gordon, R. (2012), "Is US Economic Growth Over? Faltering Innovation Confronts the Six Headwinds,"*NBER Working Paper* 18315.

[9] Gordon, R. (2016), *The Rise and Fall of American Growth*, Princeton University Press.

[10] Grossmann, G. and E. Helpman (1991), *Innovation and Growth in the World Economy*, Cambridge, MA: MIT Press.

[11] Hansen, A. (1939), "Economic Progress and declining Population Growth," *A.E.R.*29:1-15.

[12] Jones, C. (1995),"R&D-Based models of Economic Growth."*J.P.E.*103: 759-784.

[13] Jones, C. and D. Vollrath (2013), Introduction to Economic Growth (3rd Edition), W. W. Norton & Co. Inc: New York.

[14] Keynes, J. (1937), "Some Economic Consequences of Declining Population,"in *The collected Writings of John Maynard Keynes* (1973),14:124-133.

[15] Malthus, T. (1798), *An Essay on the Principle of Population,* J.Jhonson.

[16] Romer, P. (1990)."Endogenous Technological Change."*J.P.E.*98:71-102.

[17] Solow, R. (1956). "A Contribution to the Theory of Economic Growth." Q.J.E. 70: 65-94.

[18] Summers, M. (2014), "U.S. Economic Prospects: Secular Stagnation, Hysteresis, and the Zero Lower Bound*," Business Economics,*49(2):65-73.

[19] Summers, M. (2015), "Demand Side Secular Stagnation," *A.E.R,*105(59:60-65.

Chapter 4

A Development of the Image Classifier to Classify Computer Users based on Tracing Data of Keyboard Typing

Hiroyuki Dekihara
Hiroshima Shudo University, Faculty of Economic Sciences
1-1-1, Ozuka-higashi, Asaminami-ku, Hiroshima 731-3195, Japan

Toru Ochi
Osaka Institute of Technology, Computing Center
5-16-1, Omiya, Asahi-ku, Osaka 535-8585, Japan

Minori Kurahasi
Hagoromo University of International Studies
1-1, Yamadaoka, Suita, Osaka 565-0871, Japan

Masafumi Imai
Toyohashi Sozo University
20-1, Matsushita, Ushikawacho, Toyohashi, Aichi 440-8511, Japan

Abstract
We have developed a monitoring system measuring input methods: Keyboard and Flick Inputs, for developers of newer devices, researchers in ICT education, and various other related fields. Our means of measuring has adopted MediaPipe by AI Library to be able to record these movements in both the keyboard and the flick input method with an inexpensive webcam. In this research, we have developed a novel image classifier that classifies computer users by level based on tracing data of keyboard input measured using this measurement method by Machine Learning. The image classifier consists of the monitoring system and the classification model. The classification model has been built by the LightGBM. The performance of the model was evaluated in the experiment and the experimental results shows their effectiveness.

Key Words: Keyboard, Typing, Measurement, LightGBM

1. Introduction

There is a marked tendency to choose smartphones and other touch-screen devices to access the Internet rather than PCs among the younger generation [1-3]. This trend embraces the flick input method, other touch-panel-operated methods, and the speech input method. During and after COVID-19, most people use PC, tablets, and mobile devices not only for remote work and remote classes but also for business, study, and everyday life. And, students in primary, secondary, and higher education often take face-to-face or online classes while using mobile devices [4-6]. And monitoring systems for education have been developed to monitor and analyze online classes after and during COVID-19 especially [7-9]. Therefore, it is indispensable for developers of novel devices and researchers in ICT education and other related fields to collect, analyze, and feedback extensive and effective data on the actual and major patterns of input methods among PC users in order to supply new services and make further improvements. We have developed a monitoring system measuring input methods: Keyboard and Flick Inputs, for the developers and the researchers [10-12]. Our means of measuring has adopted MediaPipe [13] by AI Library to record these movements in both the keyboard and the flick input method with an inexpensive webcam. In this research, we have developed a novel image classifier that classifies computer users by level based on tracing data of keyboard input measured using this measurement method by Machine Learning. The image classifier consists of the monitoring system and the classification model. The classification model has been built by LightGBM (Light Gradient Boosting Machine) [14] which is a gradient-boosting framework that uses tree-based learning algorithms and is able to classify users into several groups based on the user's levels: typing speed, score, etc. By the information of the classified results, we are able to evaluate the proficiency and skill of users, recognize the situation of progress like class, work, etc. and give feedback to them. The performance of the model was evaluated in the experiment and the experimental results shows their effectiveness. Our image classifier and the development method of our classifier will be expected to contribute to evaluating and recognizing the actions of PC users, workers, learners, etc.

2. Proposed method

We have developed a monitoring system for recording traced data measuring the face and the hands of a user during operating PCs and smartphones. The system could detect the coordinates of landmarks in the face and hands from a captured image of the user using webcams. We have developed the image classifier to classify computer users based on the tracing data from webcams. The proposed method would be explained in the following section.

2.1 Workflow of proposed method

A workflow of our proposed method is shown in Figure 1. First, the typing skills of PC users are evaluated based on time and score of e-typing [15]. The data of users are clustered by K-Means [16, 17] which is one of the famous clustering methods aiming at partitioning the dataset by minimizing the within-cluster variance. The clusters are labeled by analysts for correct information for building a classification model. Second, the PC users are observed by our monitoring system for measuring the landmarks of the face and the hands during operating PC. Third, a classification model is built based on the labeled data by LightGBM which is a kind of supervised learning and is a gradient-boosting framework that uses tree-based learning algorithms. Finally, the image classifier is realized by combining the monitoring system and the classification model. The monitoring system and the classification model are described in sections 2.2 and 2.3.

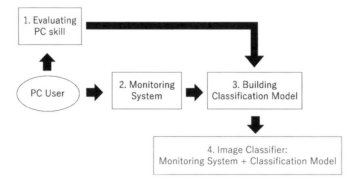

Figure 1. Workflow of the proposed method

2.2 Monitoring system

Our monitoring system consists of a PC, webcams, and AI library MediaPipe to sense landmarks of face or hands to get real-time recognition. We prepared two webcams for recording finger and hand motions in our experiment. (Figure 2) We used a webcam named Logitech C270n priced at about 20 dollars. Any type of camera for daily use is enough. The monitoring system has been developed by the two techniques: the parallel processing and the synchronization. The former is for performing multiple measurement processes of such data as camera shooting and input devices independently and in parallel. The latter is for analyzing the captured multiple data. We created a simple Text Editor as an application based on wxPython [18], which is an open-source software, in our experiment. The participant inputted the sentence on the simple Text Editor, and their motion of hands was measured by the system. Figure 3 shows the list of landmarks of Hand landmark detection [19] in MediaPipe. The Hand landmark detection is able to detect palms and perform precise key point localization of 21 2D/3D hand-knuckle coordinates inside the detected hand regions via regression. Our classification model of the image classification has been created based on 6 key points (0. WRIST, 4. THUMB_TIP, 8. INDEX_FINGER_TIP, 12. MIDDLE_FINGER_TIP, 16. RING_FINGER_TIP and 20. PINKY_TIP) of them.

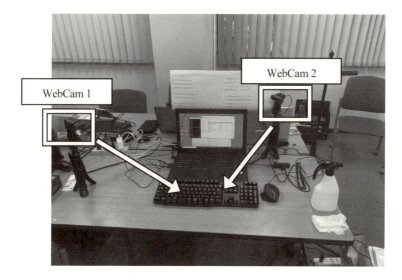

Figure 2. Overview of the monitoring system

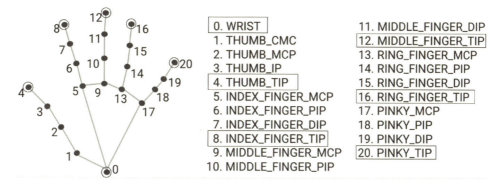

Figure 3. Example of landmarks of hand landmark detection in MediaPipe

2.3 Building classification model by LightGBM

The image classifier consists of the monitoring system and the classification model. The classification model has been built by LightGBM. The LightGBM is a kind of GBDT (Gradient Boosting Decision Tree) [20] and is designed to be distributed and efficient with some advantages, such as faster training speed and higher efficiency, lower memory usage, better accuracy, capability of handling large-scale data, and so on. And the LightGBM is one of the supervised learning which uses labeled data sets as input to train algorithms to classify data or predict outcomes. It is defined by its use of labeled data sets to train algorithms that to classify data or predict outcomes accurately. The label is defined based on each cluster of K-Means which aims to group a set of n observations into k clusters. The input data of K-Means is the time and score of users in the e-typing which is a typing application on the website. LightGBM is trained and evaluated using the labeled data set. The label is according to the proficiency of the keyboard typing in the experiment and is attached based on the result of K-Means. The results of K-Means would be shown in section 3.2.

3. Experiment

The proposed method and the experimental results would be explained in the section. We experimented at two Universities A and B in Juby 2022 and April 2023. The number of the participants at A was 18, and the experimental data was used as the train and the valid data to build the classification model of the LightGBM. The number of the participants at B was 6, and the experimental data was used as test data to evaluate the built model. The experimental conditions and the experimental results are described in sections 3.1 and 3.2.

3.1 Experimental conditions

We experimented to build the classification model and evaluate our method on the following conditions. There was a case study in the experiment: keyboard (n = 18). We attached two webcams to a Windows Laptop PC, a building webcam on the laptop for recording face orientation, and the others for each hand and finger movement (The later data were used for building and analyzing in the experiment). Then we quantified the distribution of the performance on PC skill: the keyboard typing). The typing score of participants was examined by the typing website e-typing in the keyboard experiment. Also, the monitoring system recorded the traced data of the user during typing the following 8 sentences of the 3 topics on the simple Text Editor in the monitoring system in the experiment. The overview of the experiment is shown in Figure 4.

Topic 1 (alphabets from a to z)
1) abcdefghijklmnopqrstuvwxyz
2) abcdefghijklmnopqrstuvwxyz
3) abcdefghijklmnopqrstuvwxyz

Topic 2 (pangram)
4) jumbling vext frowzy hacks pdq
5) jumbling vext frowzy hacks pdq
6) blowzy night frumps vexd jack q
7) blowzy night frumps vexd jack q

Topic 3 (Japanese)
8) 私は 広島修道大学 経済科学部 経済情報学科＿年です。
好きな授業は＿＿＿、＿＿＿、＿＿＿です。
苦手な授業は＿＿＿、＿＿＿、＿＿＿です。
(Original Japanese version)

watashiha hiroshimashudodaigaku keizaikagakubu keizaijohogakka__nendesu。
sukinajugyoha_____、_____、_____desu。
nigatenajugyoha_____、_____、_____desu。
(Original Japanese version in Roman alphabet)

I am a ____ year student in the Department of Economic Informatics, the Faculty of Economic Sciences at Hiroshima Shudo University.
My favorite classes are _____, _____, and _____.
My dislike classes are _____, _____, and _____.
(English version)

Figure 4. Overview of the experiment

3.2 Experimental results

Table 1 shows the results of time (sec.) typing the topic and the score point on the typing website e-typing each of the participants (n = 18). The data in Table 1 was set to the input dataset in K-Means (k = 3). The scatter diagram of Figure 5 illustrates the result of K-Means. The three clusters (the symbols of the square, the inverted triangle, and the cross) would be able to be recognized on the diagram and are regarded as the middle, the high, and the low levels of proficiency in PC skills. The three symbols of the circle are the centroid of each cluster. We quantified the distance d of the hand movement on the X-Y plane from the home position of the key typing each sentence. Then, the distance ratio R was calculated by dividing d by the distance between WRIST and INDEX_FINGER_TIP. For example, the bar graph of the average distance ratio R about sentence 8) on No.1 is shown in Figure 6. The movement characteristic of both hands is able to be recognized in the Fig. 6. We made the landmarks (WRIST, THUMB_TIP, INDEX_FINGER_TIP, MIDDLE_FINGER_TIP, RING_FINGER_TIP, and PINKY_TIP) of a hand the dataset A in the experiment. The dataset consisted of the label of K-Means and the 12 data (x, y) which were the landmarks of both the hands on the participants. L_WRIST, L_THUMB_TIP, L_INDEX_FINGER_TIP, L_MIDDLE_FINGER_TIP, L_RING_FINGER_TIP, and PINKY_TIP are the landmarks of the left hand. And R_WRIST, R_THUMB_TIP, R_INDEX_FINGER_TIP, R_MIDDLE_FINGER_TIP, R_RING_FINGER_TIP, and R_PINKY_TIP are the landmarks of the right hand in the Fig. 6. The dataset A was split 0.8:0.2 to the train data and the valid data.

Table 1. Time of typing the topic and score of the typing website

No	Score (pt.)	Time (sec.)	No	Score (pt.)	Time (sec.)
1	134	220.7	11	70	96.0
2	73	126.5	12	125	136.9
3	109	188.5	13	146	62.9
4	230	85.4	14	208	80.6
5	102	100.9	15	151	58.4
6	162	114.3	16	124	118.2
7	147	76.9	17	137	100.9
8	275	58.7	18	199	59.5
9	160	54.8	---	---	---
10	146	88.7	---	---	---

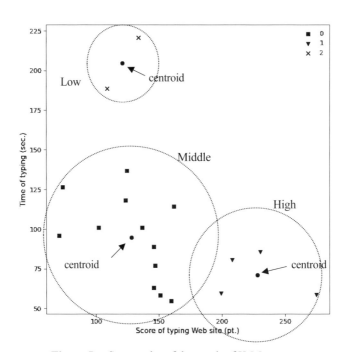

Figure 5. Scatter plot of the result of K-Means

A Development of the Image Classifier to Classify Computer Users 59

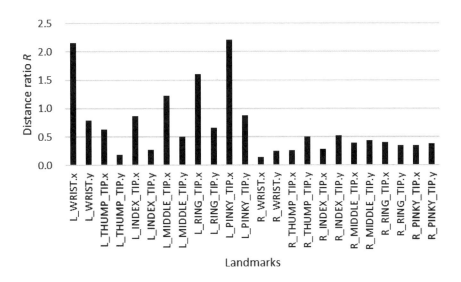

Figure 6. Bar graph of distance ratio R each hand landmarks about the sentence 8) on No. 1

The LightGBM was trained by the dataset that had 144 records {(18 participants) x (8 sentences)}. And the hyperparameters of the LightGBM were sought by the Optuna [21] which is one of the automatic hyperparameter optimization software frameworks, particularly designed for machine learning. The tuned hyperparameters are shown in Figure 7. Then, the LightGBM was trained under the conditions and the learning curves (the multi log losses of train and valid data) of the LightGBM is plotted in Figure 8. The classification report on the scikit-learn [22] Library is presented in Table 2. The accuracy of the whole model was about 90% in the validation process. The F1-scores of both High level and Middle level groups were good. On the other hand the precision of Low level groups was not well because of 0.67. Next, the feature importance in the result of LightGBM is shown in Figure 9. The action of the left hand was important in the key typing from Fig. 9 because the landmarks of the left hand (L_INDEX_TIP.y, L_WRIST.x, L_INDEX_TIP.x, L_MIDDLE_TIP.y, L_THUMP_TIP.y, L_PINKY_TIP.y, L_MIDDLE_TIP.x and L_WRIST.y) were the top 8 of the feature importance.

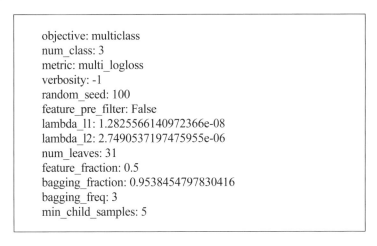

Figure 7. The tuned hyperparameters of the LightGBM

Finally, the classification model was tried to classify the independent dataset B (n = 6) from the train dataset A. The dataset B was the inputted data that the participants at University B typed the sentences similar to the sentence 8) in the section 3.1. In the case study, the accuracy was about 83%. Therefore, it was suggested that it may be possible to generalize the classification of PC users based on their actions during PC operation.

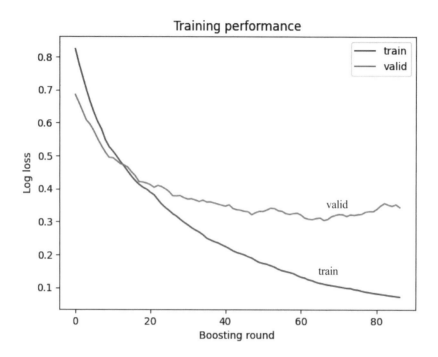

Figure 8. Graph of learning curves in the LightGBM

Table 2. The result of classification

	Precision	Recall	F1-score	Support
High	1.00	0.80	0.89	5
Middle	0.95	0.91	0.93	22
Low	0.50	1.00	0.67	2
Accuracy	---	---	0.90	29
Macro avg.	0.82	0.90	0.83	29
Weighted avg.	0.93	0.90	0.90	29

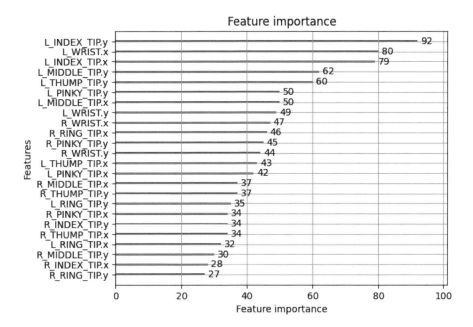

Figure 9. Horizon bar graph on the feature importance in the result of LightGBM

4. Conclusion and future plans

The image classifier has been developed to classify computer users based on the tracing data of keyboard typing in this paper. The image classifier consists of our monitoring system with our novel classification model. The model was built by the LightGBM based on the labeled dataset using K-means. We evaluated the model in the experiment. The results show the followings; the accuracy of the whole model is about 90%, the F1-scores of both on High and Middle level groups are good, and the action of the left hand is very important because the almost top of feature importance are the landmarks of the left hand.

We plan to analyze the hand motions each key and conduct further experiments with larger numbers of people in the future.

Acknowledgements

This work was supported by JSPS KAKENHI Grant Number 20K12100.

References

[1] Consumer Affairs Agency, "White Paper on Consumer Affairs 2022," (2022).
[2] Ministry of Internal Affairs and Communications, "2022 White Paper on Information and Communications in Japan," (2022).
[3] Radesky, Jenny S et al., "Young Children's Use of Smartphones and Tablets," Pediatrics vol.146, No.1 (2020).

[4] Ministry of Education, Culture, Sports, Science and Technology, "White Paper on Science and Technology 2020," (2020).
[5] Liu, Xixi, "The Effects of Tablet Use on Student Learning Achievements, Participation, and Motivation at Different Levels," *International Journal of Technology-Enhanced Education*, Vol.1, No.1, pp.1-17 (2022).
[6] Hiraoka, S.,Nishi, M., "A Study of Keyboard Skills of University and High School Students", *Shinshu University Journal of Educational Research and Practice*, No.11, pp.181-190 (2017).
[7] Yousun KANG, Hiroyuki KAMBARA, and Duk SHIN, "Evaluation of Concentration Levels in Online Learning Using an Eye Tracker Device," *Journal of the Institute of Image Electronics Engineers of Japan*, Vol.51, No.2, pp.164-169 (2022).
[8] Händel, M., Bedenlier, S., Kopp, B. et al., "The webcam and student engagement in synchronous online learning: visually or verbally?," Educ Inf Technol 27, 10405–10428 (2022).
[9] Rajab, Mohammad H, and Mohammed Soheib, "Privacy Concerns Over the Use of Webcams in Online Medical Education During the COVID-19 Pandemic," Cureus, Vol.13, No.2 (2021).
[10] Ochi T, Kurahasi M, Dekihara H, Imai M. and Kuramoto A., "A Proposal for Constructing Multi-Dimensional Measurement Environment for Input Interfaces: How Do the College students in the Smartphone Generation Use Them?", IPSJ Information Education Symposium, Vol. 2019, pp. 214-219 (2019).
[11] Ochi, T., Kurahasi, M., Imai, M., Dekihara, H. & Kuramoto, A, "A Proposal of a Means of Measurement for the Assessment of Two Types of Input Methods: Keyboard Input and Flick Input", Proceedings of Innovate Learning Summit 2021, pp. 65-70 (2021).
[12] Toru Ochi, Minori Kurahasi, Masafumi Imai, Hiroyuki Dekihara, Atsuko Kuramoto: "A Proposal for the Improved Version of a Means of Measurement for the Assessment of Two Types of Input Methods: Keyboard Input and Flick Input," Economic History, Flow of Funds, Information Systems and Operations Research, Kyushu University Press, pp.53-67, 2023.
[13] MediaPipe, https://ai.google.dev/edge/mediapipe/solutions/guide, Google, Inc., 2024.
[14] Guolin Ke, Qi Meng, Thomas Finley, Taifeng Wang, Wei Chen, Weidong Ma, Qiwei Ye, and Tie-Yan Liu. 2017. Lightgbm: A Highly Efficient Gradient Boosting Decision Tree. Advances in neural information processing systems 30 (2017).
[15] e-typing, https://www.e-typing.ne.jp/, e-typing, Inc., 2024.
[16] Macqueen, J., "Some Methods of Classification and Analysis of Multivariate Observations", Proceedings of the Fifth Berkeley Symposium on Mathematical Statistics and Probability, University of California Press, pp.281–297 (1967).
[17] Hartigan, J. A., Clustering Algorithms, John Wiley and Sons (1975)
[18] wxPyton, https://www.wxpython.org/, The wxPython Team, 2024.
[19] Hand landmarks detection guide, https://ai.google.dev/edge/mediapipe/solutions/vision/hand_landmarker, Google, Inc., 2024.
[20] Jerome H Friedman, "Greedy function approximation: a gradient boosting machine", Annals of statistics, pp.1189–1232 (2001).
[21] Optuna, https://optuna.org/, Preferred Networks, Inc., 2024.
[22] Pedregosa et al., "Scikit-learn: Machine Learning in Python," JMLR 12, pp. 2825-2830 (2011).

Chapter 5

Flat Plumbing Basket, Self-linking Number and Thurston-Bennequin Number

Keiji Tagami
Faculty of Economics Sciences, Hiroshima Shudo University,
1-1-1, Ozukahigashi, Asaminami-ku, Hiroshima, 731-3195, JAPAN

Abstract

A knot is an embedded circle into the three sphere S^3. A link is a disjoint (may not split) union of some knots. Specialists on knot and link theory are interested in relations among knots and 2-, 3- or 4-dimensional geometry. In this work, we focus on surfaces, which are 2-dimensional manifolds, whose boundaries yield links.

An oriented surface is a Seifert surface of a link if its boundary is the link. Moreover, a Seifert surface is a flat plumbing basket if it is consisting a disk and finitely many bands which are contained in distinct pages of the "trivial open book decomposition" of S^3. In this paper, we construct a Legendrian link from a flat plumbing basket, and we describe a relation between the flat plumbing basket number, which is the minimal number of the bands of flat plumbing baskets whose boundaries are the link, and some contact invariants for the Legendrian link, for example, the self-linking number or the Thurston-Bennequin number. As a corollary, we determine the flat plumbing basket numbers of torus links.

Keywords: knot, flat plumbing basket, contact structure

1 Introduction

It is well known that for any oriented link L in the 3-sphere S^3, there is some oriented compact surface whose boundary is the link L. Such a surface is called a Seifert surface of L. Furihata-Hirasawa-Kobayashi [6] introduced a concept of positions of a Seifert surface, which is called a "flat plumbing basket."

A Seifert surface is a *flat plumbing basket* if it is obtained from a disk by plumbing some unknotted and untwisted annuli so that the gluing regions are in the disk. Flat plumbing baskets can be expressed in terms of the trivial open book decomposition O of S^3. Namely, a flat plumbing basket consists of a page D_0 of O and finitely many bands which are contained in distinct pages of O.

We say that an oriented link L admits a flat plumbing basket presentation F if F is a flat plumbing basket and its boundary is L. As mentioned in the following theorem, any link is realized as the boundary of a flat plumbing basket.

Theorem 1.1 ([6])**.** *Any oriented link admits a flat plumbing basket presentation.*

On flat plumbing baskets, there are some related works (for example, see [3, 6, 9, 11, 13, 14, 15]). In particular, in [13], the concept of the flat plumbing basket number of a link is introduced. The *flat plumbing basket number* $fpbk(L)$ of an oriented link L is the minimal number of bands to obtain a flat plumbing basket presentation of the link. Hirose-Nakashima [9] gave a lower bound for $fpbk(K)$ of a knot K as follows.

Theorem 1.2 ([9, Theorem 1.3]). *Let K be a non-trivial knot, and $g(K)$ be the minimal genus of the Seifert surface (i.e. three genus) of K. For the Alexander polynomial $\Delta_K(t)$ of K, let a be the coefficient of the term of highest degree, and*

$$\deg \Delta_K(t) := (\text{the highest degree of } \Delta_K(t)) - (\text{the lowest degree of } \Delta_K(t)).$$

Then $fpbk(K)$ is evaluated as follows.

1. *If $a = \pm 1$, then $fpbk(K) \geq 2g(K) + 2$.*
2. *If $a \neq \pm 1$, then $fpbk(K) \geq \max\{2g(K) + 2, \deg \Delta_K(t) + 4\}$.*

As mentioned above, flat plumbing baskets can be expressed in terms of an open book decomposition. On the other hand, by Thurston-Winkelnkemper's work [23], we can construct a contact structure of $\mathbf{S}^3$ from an open book decomposition. Hence, it seems that there are some relations between flat plumbing baskets and contact topology.

In this paper, we construct a Legendrian link $\mathcal{L}_F$ from a flat plumbing basket F (see Section 3). This Legendrian link $\mathcal{L}_F$ is completely the same as the Legendrian link introduced in [12]. In particular, in [12], front projections of $\mathcal{L}_F$ are given. In this manuscript, we will construct $\mathcal{L}_F$ more geometrically. By utilizing this Legendrian link, we give two inequalities on flat plumbing basket numbers as follows.

Theorem 1.3 (see also [12, Theorem 1.1]). *Let L be a non-trivial oriented link in $\mathbf{S}^3$. Then we have*

$$\max\{-\overline{sl}(L), -\overline{sl}(\overline{L})\} - 1 \leq fpbk(L),$$

where $\overline{L}$ is the mirror image of L and $\overline{sl}(L)$ is the maximal self-linking number of L (for detail see Section 4 and Theorem 4.1).

Theorem 1.4. *Let L be a non-trivial oriented link in $\mathbf{S}^3$. Suppose that L has no split component which is isotopic to the unknot. Then, we obtain*

$$\max\{-\overline{tb}(L), -\overline{tb}(\overline{L})\} + 2 \leq 2fpbk(L),$$

where $\overline{tb}(L)$ is the maximal Thurston-Bennequin number of L. The equality holds if and only if L is a non-trivial alternating torus link $T_{2,n}$ for some $|n| \geq 2$.

The author remarks that a generalization of Theorem 1.4 has been given in [12, Theorem 1.2]. Here, a proof for Theorem 1.4, which is compatible with our construction of $\mathcal{L}_F$, will be introduced. As a corollary, we determine $fpbk(T_{p,q})$ for the (p,q)-torus link $T_{p,q}$ (see Corollary 4.2). Moreover, by using Theorems 1.3 and 1.4, we improve [9, Table 1] (see Table 1).

1.1 Organization

This paper is organized as follows: In Section 2, we recall the definitions of open book decompositions, flat plumbing baskets and contact structures. In Section 3, we construct a Legendrian link from a flat plumbing basket. Moreover, we describe a relation among the maximal self-linking numbers, the maximal Thurston-Bennequin numbers and the flat plumbing basket numbers. In Section 4, we prove Theorem 1.3 (Theorem 4.1). In Section 5, we prove Theorem 1.4. In Section 6, we give further observations.

This paper is a reorganized version of a preprint arXiv:1709.08837.

2 Preliminary

2.1 Trivial Open Book Decomposition and Flat Plumbing Basket

Let M be an oriented closed 3-manifold. Suppose that for a link L in M, there is a fiber projection $\pi : M \setminus L \to \mathbf{S}^1$ such that each fiber is the interior of a Seifert surface of L. Then, (L, π) is called an *open book decomposition* of M. The closure of each fiber is called a *page*, and L is called the *binding*.

Let U be the unknot in $\mathbf{S}^3$. The knot complement $\mathbf{S}^3 \setminus U$ is homeomorphic to the product $\text{Int}(D^2) \times \mathbf{S}^1$. Hence, there exists a fiber projection $\pi \colon \mathbf{S}^3 \setminus U \to \mathbf{S}^1$ whose fibers $\pi^{-1}(\theta)$ are open disks for $0 \le \theta < 2\pi$. Put $D_\theta := \overline{\pi^{-1}(\theta)}$. An orientation of U induces an orientation of each fiber D_θ and a positive direction of the fibration $\{D_\theta\}_{0 \le \theta < 2\pi}$ (see Figure 1). This fibration is called the *trivial open book decomposition* of $\mathbf{S}^3$, denoted by O. Then, the unknot is the binding, and each D_θ is a page of O. Throughout this paper, we consider the trivial open book decomposition.

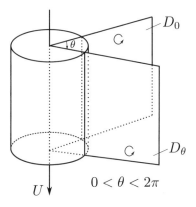

Figure 1: Open book decomposition

A Seifert surface F is a *flat plumbing basket* if there are finitely many bands $B_1, \ldots, B_n$ and $0 < \theta_1 < \cdots < \theta_n < 2\pi$ such that $F = D_0 \cup B_1 \cup \cdots \cup B_n$, each band B_i is contained in D_{θ_i} and $B_i \cap U$ consists of two arcs. We call the subscript i of B_i the *label* of the band. A flat plumbing basket F is a *flat plumbing basket presentation* of an oriented link L if ∂F is ambient isotopic to L (for example, see Figure 2).

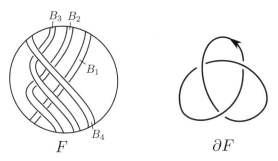

Figure 2: An example of a flat plumbing basket F. It is a flat plumbing presentation of the negative trefoil. The flat basket code is $W_F = (1, 2, 3, 4, 1, 2, 3, 4)$.

For a flat plumbing basket F, by recording the labels of the bands as one travels along $U = \partial D_0$, one obtains a cyclic word W_F in $\{1, \ldots, n\}$ such that each letter appears exactly twice, where n is the number of bands of F. We call W_F the *flat basket code for F*.

We define the *flat plumbing basket number* $fpbk(L)$ of an oriented link L to be the minimal number of bands to obtain a flat plumbing basket presentation of L from D_0. In other words,

$$fpbk(L) := \min\{b_1(F) \mid F \text{ is a flat plumbing basket presentation of } L\},$$

where $b_1(F)$ is the first betti number of F. We remark that $fpbk(L) \in 2\mathbf{Z} + |L| - 1$, where $|L|$ is the number of the components of L, and $fpbk$ is preserved under taking mirror image.

2.2 Trivial Open Book Decomposition and Standard Contact Structure

In this section, we recall the relation between open book decompositions and contact structures. For detail, for example, see [19].

Let M be an oriented closed 3-manifold. A 1-form $\alpha \in \Omega^1(M)$ is a *contact form* if $\alpha \wedge d\alpha$ is nowhere 0. A 2-dimensional distribution $\xi \subset TM$ is a *contact structure* if there is a contact form α such that $\xi = \operatorname{Ker} \alpha$. A contact structure ξ on M is *supported* by an open book decomposition (L, π) if ξ can be represented by a contact form α such that the binding is a transverse to ξ, $d\alpha$ is a volume form on every page and the orientation of binding induced by α agrees with the orientations of the pages.

It is known that for any open book decomposition of M, we can construct a contact structure on M supported by the open book decomposition by Thurston-Winkelnkemper's construction [23]. By Giroux's work [8], such a contact structure is unique up to contact isotopy. In particular, the trivial open book decomposition O of $\mathbf{S}^3$ supports the standard contact structure $\xi_{std} = \operatorname{Ker}(dz + r^2 d\theta)$ of $\mathbf{S}^3$, which is contact isotopic to $\operatorname{Ker}(dz + xdy)$. See Figure 3.

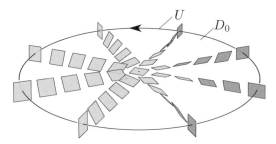

Figure 3: A schematic picture of the standard contact structure ξ_{std} on $\mathbf{S}^3$. The boundary corresponds to $r = \infty$.

For a surface Σ in $\mathbf{S}^3$, we consider $\xi_{std} \cap T\Sigma$. For generic Σ, this intersection is a line field except at finitely many points where Σ is tangent to ξ_{std}. By integrating $\xi_{std} \cap T\Sigma$, we obtain a foliation [1] of Σ with singularities. Such a foliation is called the *characteristic foliation* of Σ in ξ_{std}. In the next section, Section 3, we will construct a Legendrian link $\mathcal{L}_F$ from a flat plumbing basket F, which is isotopic to the boundary ∂F. Then, it is convenient to see the characteristic foliation of the boundary of a tubular neighborhood of U and each fiber D_θ (see Figures 4 and 5).

---

[1] A *foliation* of a manifold is a decomposition into submanifolds. Each submanifold is called *leaf*.

Figure 4: Characteristic foliation of D_0. This characteristic foliation has one singular point. The characteristic foliations of other fibers D_θ are similar to that of D_0. In particular there is one singular point.

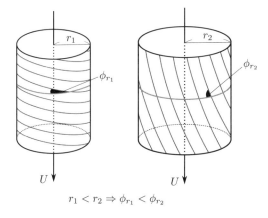

$r_1 < r_2 \Rightarrow \phi_{r_1} < \phi_{r_2}$

Figure 5: Characteristic foliation of the boundary of a tubular neighborhood of the binding U. If we increase the radius of the tube, then the angle ϕ_r between the foliation and the meridian also increases.

3 Legendrian Link from Flat Plumbing Basket

Let $\mathcal{L}$ be an oriented link in $\mathbf{S}^3$. Then, $\mathcal{L}$ is a *Legendrian link* in ξ_{std} if it is tangent to ξ_{std}. In this section, we construct a Legendrian link from a flat plumbing basket.

Let F be a flat plumbing basket with $b_1(F) > 0$. Let $N(U)$ be a tubular neighborhood of the binding U. Since U is transverse to ξ_{std}, the boundary ∂F is not a Legendrian link. However, since each page is "almost" tangent to ξ_{std}, we can regard $\partial F \setminus N(U)$ as a disjoint union of Legendrian arcs. More precisely, we can approximate each component of $\partial F \setminus N(U)$ by a Legendrian arc without changing the link type of ∂F. To see this, we thin each band B_i sufficiently, and we move the band without moving $B_i \cap U$ so that the core of B_i is on two leaves of the characteristic foliation of D_{θ_i} (see Figure 6). Then, there is a small perturbation (isotopy) $f_t : \mathbf{S}^3 \to \mathbf{S}^3$ such that $f_0 = \mathrm{id}$ and $f_1(\partial B_i \setminus N(U))$ is Legendrian (by Legendrian realization principle [10]). After this operation, $\partial B_i \setminus N(U)$ can be regarded as Legendrian arcs.

As mentioned above, we see that $\partial F \cap N(U)$ is not Legendrian. In order to construct a Legendrian link from ∂F, we replace each component β of $\partial F \cap N(U)$ by an arc α depicted in Figure 7. Each α is in a leaf of the characteristic foliation of $\partial(N(U))$, connects the two points of $\partial \beta$ and satisfies $|\alpha \cap D_0| = 1$. We can take such an α by adjusting the radius of $N(U)$ locally.

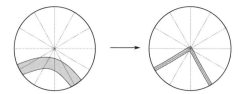

Figure 6: Thinning and moving a band B_i so that the core of B_i is on two leaves of the characteristic foliation of D_{θ_i}.

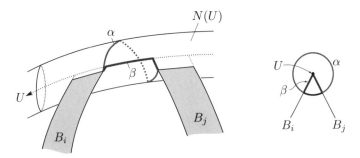

Figure 7: In order to construct a Legendrian link $\mathcal{L}_F$ from ∂F, we replace each component β of $\partial F \cap N(U)$ by an arc α. The arc α is contained in a leaf of the characteristic foliation of $\partial(N(U))$ (see Figure 5), connects the two points of $\partial \beta$ and satisfies $|\alpha \cap D_0| = 1$. By adjusting the radius of $N(U)$ locally, we can take such an α.

By this replacement (and smoothing the curve at the points of $\partial F \cap \partial(N(U))$ in ξ_{std}), we obtain a Legendrian link from ∂F. We denote the Legendrian link by $\mathcal{L}_F$, and called the *Legendrian link associated with F*. For example, see Figure 8.

The classical invariants, the Thurston-Bennequin number tb and the rotation number rot, of $\mathcal{L}_F$ can be computed as follows.

Lemma 3.1. *Let F be a flat plumbing basket with $b_1(F) > 0$ and $\mathcal{L}_F$ be the Legendrian link associated with F. Then, we obtain*

$$tb(\mathcal{L}_F) = -2b_1(F),$$

where $tb(\mathcal{L}_F)$ is the Thurston-Bennequin number of $\mathcal{L}_F$.

Proof. Let $\mathcal{L}_F^+$ be a Legendrian link obtained by pushing of $\mathcal{L}_F$ in the direction of a nonzero vector field transverse to ξ_{std}. Then the Thurston-Bennequin number $tb(\mathcal{L}_F)$ is computed by

$$tb(\mathcal{L}_F) = lk(\mathcal{L}_F, \mathcal{L}_F^+),$$

where $lk(\mathcal{L}_F, \mathcal{L}_F^+)$ is the linking number between $\mathcal{L}_F$ and $\mathcal{L}_F^+$. By Figure 9, we see that each band of F contributes -2 to the linking number. Note that the crossings between two distinct bands do not contribute the linking number. Since $b_1(F)$ is equal to the number of the bands of the flat plumbing basket F, we finish the proof. □

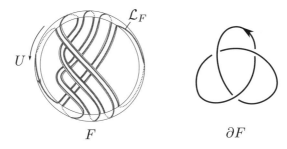

Figure 8: An example of $\mathcal{L}_F$. This is isotopic to the negative trefoil knot. Precisely, the radius of $N(U)$ is non-uniform.

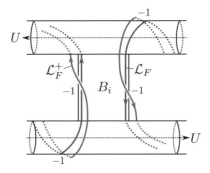

Figure 9: Near a band of a flat plumbing basket. Each band contributes $-4/2 = -2$ to the linking number $lk(\mathcal{L}_F, \mathcal{L}_F^+)$.

Lemma 3.2. *Let F be a flat plumbing basket with $b_1(F) > 0$ and $\mathcal{L}_F$ be the Legendrian link associated with F. Suppose that $\mathcal{L}_F$ has the orientation which agrees with the orientation of the binding U. Then, we obtain*

$$rot(\mathcal{L}_F) = -b_1(F) + 1,$$

where $rot(\mathcal{L}_F)$ is the rotation number of $\mathcal{L}_F$.

Proof. The rotation number $rot(\mathcal{L})$ of an oriented Legendrian link $\mathcal{L}$ is the winding number of $T\mathcal{L}$ with respect to a trivialization of ξ_{std} along $\mathcal{L}$. Let $W_F = (i_1, i_2, \ldots, i_{2n})$ be the flat basket code of F, where $n = b_1(F)$. For convenience, define $i_{2n+1} = i_1$. Let α be the arc in $\mathcal{L}_F$ which connects B_{i_k} and $B_{i_{k+1}}$ as in Figure 10. Define ζ_k be the angle corresponding to the arc in U which connects B_{i_k} and $B_{i_{k+1}}$. Then, as in Figure 10, the arc α contributes

$$-2\pi + (\theta_{i_{k+1}} - \theta_{i_k}) + \frac{\pi}{2} \times 2 + \zeta_k$$

to $2\pi \times rot(\mathcal{L}_F)$. Moreover, when we go across a band B_i twice along $\mathcal{L}_F$, the winding number increases ξ_i, where ξ_i is the angle corresponding to the two arcs in $B_i \cap U$ (see Figure 11). Then, we obtain

$$2\pi \times rot(\mathcal{L}_F) = \sum_{k=1}^{2n}(-2\pi + (\theta_{i_{k+1}} - \theta_{i_k}) + \frac{\pi}{2} \times 2 + \zeta_k) + \sum_{i=1}^{n} \xi_i$$
$$= -2n\pi + \left(\sum_{k=1}^{2n} \zeta_k + \sum_{i=1}^{n} \xi_i\right)$$
$$= -2n\pi + 2\pi.$$

Hence, we have $rot(\mathcal{L}_F) = -n + 1 = -b_1(F) + 1$. □

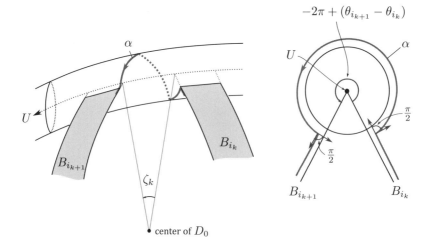

Figure 10: Contribution of α to the rotation number of $\mathcal{L}_F$

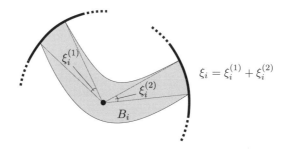

Figure 11: Contribution of band B_i to the rotation number of $\mathcal{L}_F$

4 Maximal Self-linking Number and Flat Plumbing Basket

Let l be an oriented link in $\mathbf{S}^3$. Then, l is a *transverse link* in ξ_{std} if it is positively transverse to ξ_{std}. The *self-linking number* $sl(l)$ of l is defined as the linking number $lk(l, l')$ of l and l', where l' is a push-off of l obtained by a non-zero vector field in ξ_{std}. It is known that for any Legendrian link $\mathcal{L}$, by pushing $\mathcal{L}$ in a sufficiently small annulus neighborhood, we can construct two transverse link l_+ and l_- such that $l_\pm$ is isotopic to $\mathcal{L}$ topologically and

$$sl(l_\pm) = tb(\mathcal{L}) \mp rot(\mathcal{L}).$$

For example, see [7, 19].

Let F be a flat plumbing basket with $b_1(F) > 0$ and $\partial F = L$. Let $\mathcal{L}_F$ be the Legendrian link associated with F. By Lemmas 3.1 and 3.2, we can construct a transverse link l_F such that l_F is isotopic to L and

$$sl(l_F) = tb(\mathcal{L}_F) + |rot(\mathcal{L}_F)| = -b_1(F) - 1 \in 2\mathbf{Z} + |L|.$$

Hence, we obtain the following.

Theorem 4.1 (Theorem 1.3). *Let L be a non-trivial oriented link in $\mathbf{S}^3$. Define the maximal self-linking number $sl(L)$ of L as*

$$\overline{sl}(L) := \max\{tb(\mathcal{L}) + |rot(\mathcal{L})| \mid \mathcal{L} \text{ is a Legendrian link in } \xi_{std} \text{ and isotopic to } L\}.$$

Then we have

$$\max\{-\overline{sl}(L), -\overline{sl}(\overline{L})\} - 1 \leq fpbk(L) = fpbk(\overline{L}),$$

where $\overline{L}$ is the mirror image of L.

Corollary 4.2. *For any $p \geq q > 1$, we have*

$$pq - p + q - 1 = -\overline{sl}(T_{p,-q}) - 1 = fpbk(T_{p,q}),$$

where $T_{p,q}$ is the positive (p,q)-torus link and $T_{p,-q} = \overline{T_{p,q}}$.

Proof. By Morton-Franks-Williams (MFW) inequality [5, 16], we have

$$-2b(L) \leq \overline{sl}(L) + \overline{sl}(\overline{L}) \leq -\text{breadth}_v P_L(v, z) - 2,$$

where $b(L)$ is the braid index of L and $P_L(v, z)$ is the HOMFLYPT polynomial. Franks and Williams [5] proved that for any torus link, MFW inequality is sharp, that is

$$2q = \text{breadth}_v P_{T_{p,q}}(v, z) + 2.$$

Moreover, it is known that $\overline{sl}(T_{p,q}) = pq - p - q$ ([1]). Hence, we have

$$-\overline{sl}(T_{p,-q}) \geq \overline{sl}(T_{p,q}) + \text{breadth}_v P_{T_{p,q}}(v, z) + 2 = pq - p + q.$$

On the other hand, by [6, Theorem 2.4], we see that $T_{p,q}$ has a flat plumbing basket presentation F with $b_1(F) = pq - p + q - 1$. By Theorem 4.1, we have

$$-\overline{sl}(T_{p,-q}) \leq fpbk(T_{p,q}) + 1 \leq pq - p + q,$$

and we finish the proof. □

Remark 4.3. In [12, Theorem 3.6], Ito and the author proved that the equality of Theorem 1.4 holds for positive braid links, which is the class containing all torus links. In particular, [12, Theorem 3.6] contains Corollary 4.2.

Corollary 4.4. *Let L be an oriented link with $\overline{sl}(L) = -\chi(L)$, where $\chi(L)$ is the maximal Euler characteristic of L (for example, if L is strongly quasipositive, L satisfies this condition). Then we have*

$$1 - \chi(L) + \text{breadth}_v P_L(v, z) \leq fpbk(L).$$

Proof. By MFW inequality and Theorem 4.1, we have

$$\overline{sl}(L) + \text{breadth}_v\, P_L(v,z) + 2 \leq -\overline{sl}(\overline{L}) \leq fpbk(L) + 1.$$

By the assumption, we finish the proof. □

Corollary 4.5. *Let L be an oriented link. Then, we have*

$$\text{maxdeg}_v\, P_L(v,z) \leq -\overline{sl}(L) - 1 \leq fpbk(L).$$

Proof. The first inequality is the HOMFLYPT bound on the self-linking number, which follows from MFW inequality. The second follows from Theorem 4.1. □

Corollary 4.6. *Let K_m be the m-twist knot (Figure 12). Then, for any $k \geq 0$, we have $2k \leq fpbk(K_{2k})$ and $2k + 4 \leq fpbk(K_{2k+1})$.*

Proof. By [4, Theorem 1.2], we see that

- $\max\{-\overline{sl}(K_{2k}), -\overline{sl}(\overline{K_{2k}})\} \geq 2k + 1$,
- $\max\{-\overline{sl}(K_{2k+1}), -\overline{sl}(\overline{K_{2k+1}})\} \geq 2k + 5$.

By Theorem 4.1, we finish the proof. □

Remark 4.7. Mikami Hirasawa showed that $fpbk(K_{2k+1}) \leq 2k + 4$ for $k \geq 0$, and $fpbk(K_{2k}) \leq 2k$ for $k \geq 3$ in private communication. Hence, by Corollary 4.6, we have

- $fpbk(K_{2k+1}) = 2k + 4$ for $k \geq 0$,
- $fpbk(K_{2k}) = 2k$ for $k \geq 3$,
- $fpbk(K_2) = 4$ and $fpbk(K_4) = 6$.

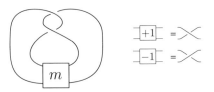

Figure 12: The *m*-twist knot K_m

Example 4.8. By Corollary 4.2, we have

$$fpbk(3_1) = 4 = \text{maxdeg}_v\, P_{3_1}(v,z).$$

Moreover, since the right-hand side is additive and $fpbk$ is subadditive under connected sum, by Corollary 4.5, we have

$$fpbk(\sharp_n 3_1) = 4n.$$

5 Maximal Thurston-Bennequin Number and Flat Plumbing Basket

Let L be an oriented link in $\mathbf{S}^3$. The *maximal Thurston-Bennequin number* $\overline{tb}(L)$ of L is the maximal number of Thurston-Bennequin numbers of Legendrian links in ξ_{std} which are isotopic to L. In this section, we compare $tb(\mathcal{L}_F)$ with $\overline{tb}(L)$, where $L = \partial F$.

Let α be an arc used in the construction of $\mathcal{L}_F$. Suppose that α goes round the meridian of $\partial(N(U))$. See the left picture of Figure 13. If we increase the radius of $N(U)$, the angle between the characteristic foliation and the meridian also increases as in Figure 5. Hence, by increasing the radius of $N(U)$ locally, we can obtain a new Legendrian arc α' instead of α (see Figure 13). Then, we can construct a new Legendrian link by replacing α in $\mathcal{L}_F$ with α' as in Figure 13. We call this operation a *shortcut* for $\mathcal{L}_F$. By considering the Lagrangian projection, we see that a shortcut corresponds to a (de)stabilization in a Lagrangian projection of $\mathcal{L}_F$.

Lemma 5.1. *Let F be a flat plumbing basket. Let $\mathcal{L}'_F$ be a Legendrian link obtained from $\mathcal{L}_F$ by taking one shortcut. Then, we obtain $tb(\mathcal{L}'_F) = tb(\mathcal{L}_F) + 1$.*

Proof. See Figure 14. □

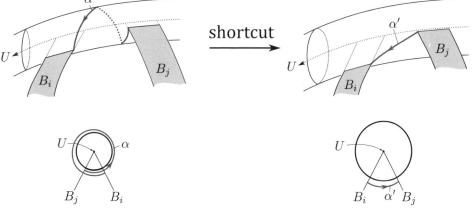

Figure 13: Shortcut operation. In this picture, $j > i$, that is, $\theta_j > \theta_i$ (cf. Figure 7). In this case, we can take a shortcut. Namely we can replace α with α'.

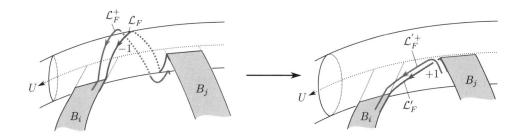

Figure 14: One shortcut contributes $(+1 - (-1))/2 = +1$ to the Thurston-Bennequin number.

Lemma 5.2. *Let F be a flat plumbing basket with $b_1(F) = n \geq 2$. Suppose that ∂F has no split component which is isotopic to the unknot. Then, we can take at least two shortcuts for $\mathcal{L}_F$.*

Proof. Let W_F be the flat basket code of F. Because ∂F has no split component which is isotopic to the unknot, W_F has no subcode (n, n). Since the cyclic word W_F has exactly two n, there are two subcodes (n, i_1) and (n, i_2) of W_F for some $i_1, i_2 \in \{1, \ldots, n-1\}$. At the corresponding places in F to subcodes (n, i_1) and (n, i_2), we can take shortcuts for $\mathcal{L}_F$ since $n > i_1$ and $n > i_2$. □

By Lemmas 3.1, 5.1 and 5.2, we obtain the following.

Lemma 5.3. *Let L be a non-trivial oriented link. Suppose that L has no split component which is isotopic to the unknot. Then, we obtain*

$$-\overline{tb}(L) + 2 \leq 2fpbk(L).$$

Proof. Let F be a flat plumbing basket presentation of L with $b_1(F) = fpbk(L)$. By Lemma 3.1, we have $tb(\mathcal{L}_F) = -2b_1(F)$. By Lemmas 5.1 and 5.2, we obtain $tb(\mathcal{L}_F) \leq \overline{tb}(L) - 2$. Hence, we have $-\overline{tb}(L) + 2 \leq 2b_1(F)$. This implies $-\overline{tb}(L) + 2 \leq 2fpbk(L)$. □

Example 5.4. Let F be the flat plumbing basket depicted in Figure 2, which presents the negative trefoil knot. The Legendrian link $\mathcal{L}_F$ associated with F is as in Figure 8. Its Thurston-Bennequin number $tb(\mathcal{L}_F)$ is -8. We can take 2 shortcuts for $tb(\mathcal{L}_F)$. Hence, $tb(\mathcal{L}_F) + 2 \leq \overline{tb}(3_1)$. It is known that $\overline{tb}(3_1) = -6$. We see that the Legendrian link obtained by taking 2 shortcuts for $\mathcal{L}_F$ attains the maximal Thurston-Bennequin number of 3_1. Moreover, we obtain

$$8 = -\overline{tb}(3_1) + 2 \leq 2fpbk(3_1) \leq 2 \times 4 = 8.$$

Hence, we have $fpbk(3_1) = 4$. This coincides the result of Example 4.8.

On the equality of Lemma 5.3, we obtain the following.

Lemma 5.5. *Let L be a non-trivial oriented link. Suppose that L has no split component which is isotopic to the unknot. Then, L satisfies*

$$-\overline{tb}(L) + 2 = 2fpbk(L)$$

if and only if L is a negative alternating torus link $\overline{T_{2,n}}$ for some $n \geq 2$.

Proof. Suppose that L satisfies $-\overline{tb}(L) + 2 = 2fpbk(L)$. Let F be a flat plumbing basket presentation of L with $b_1(F) = fpbk(L)$. Then, by Lemma 3.1, we have $tb(\mathcal{L}_F) = -2b_1(F) = -2fpbk(L) = \overline{tb}(L) - 2$. By Lemmas 5.1 and 5.2, we can take exactly two shortcuts for $\mathcal{L}_F$. Such a flat plumbing basket is depicted in Figure 15 and its boundary is a negative alternating torus link $\overline{T_{2,n}}$ for some $n \geq 2$.

Conversely, suppose that $L = \overline{T_{2,n}}$ for some $n \geq 2$. It is known that $\overline{tb}(\overline{T_{2,n}}) = -2n$ (for example, see [17]). Moreover, by Figure 15, $\overline{T_{2,n}}$ has a flat plumbing basket presentation F with $b_1(F) = n + 1$. Hence, we obtain $2n + 2 = -\overline{tb}(L) + 2 = 2fpbk(L) \leq 2(n+1)$. This implies the equality. □

Proof of Theorem 1.4. Note that $fpbk(L) = fpbk(\overline{L})$, where $\overline{L}$ is the mirror image. Hence, Theorem 1.4 follows from Lemmas 5.3 and 5.5. □

Corollary 5.6. *Let L be a non-trivial oriented link. Suppose that L has no split component which is isotopic to the unknot. If L is not an alternating torus link, we obtain*

$$\max\{-\overline{tb}(L), -\overline{tb}(\overline{L})\} + 3 \leq 2fpbk(L).$$

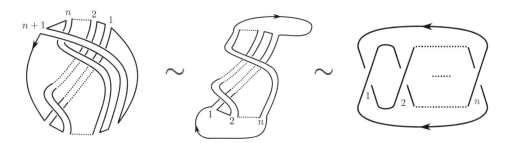

Figure 15: A flat plumbing basket presentation with $n+1$ bands. The flat basket code is $(1, 2, \cdots, n+1, 1, 2, \cdots, n+1)$. We can take exactly two shortcuts for the associated Legendrian link. The boundary is isotopic to the negative torus link $\overline{T_{2,n}}$.

Question 5.7. *When does the equality of Corollary 5.6 hold? Classify such links.*

For example, by Table 1, 8_{21} satisfies

$$\max\{-\overline{tb}(8_{21}), -\overline{tb}(\overline{8_{21}})\} + 3 = 2fpbk(8_{21}).$$

6 Further Discussion

6.1 Negativity of Links and Flat Plumbing Basket Number

It is known that the maximal self-linking number $\overline{sl}(L)$ and the maximal Thurston-Bennequin number $\overline{tb}(L)$ of a positive link L hold the equality of the Bennequin inequality [1], that is, $\overline{sl}(L) = \overline{tb}(L) = -\chi(L)$ (for example, see [22]). In this sense, $\overline{sl}$ and $\overline{tb}$ of a positive link are large. On the other hand, as corollaries of MFW inequality and the Rasmussen bound on the maximal Thurston-Bennequin number [20, 21], we obtain

$$\overline{sl}(L) + \overline{sl}(\overline{L}) \le -\text{breadth}_v\, P_L(v,z) - 2,$$
$$\overline{tb}(L) + \overline{tb}(\overline{L}) \le -2.$$

Hence, we see that the maximal self-linking number and the maximal Thurston-Bennequin number of a negative link are small. By this observation, it seems that Theorem 1.3 (or Corollary 4.5) and Theorem 1.4 (or Lemma 5.3) are effective for negative links. In particular, in Table 1, we see that $-\overline{sl}(L) - 1 = fpbk(L)$ for negative links L with up to 9 crossings.

Question 6.1. *For any negative link L, does the following hold?*

$$-\overline{sl}(L) - 1 = fpbk(L).$$

6.2 Non-Sharpness of Theorem 1.4

For any $M > 0$, there is a link L such that

$$2fpbk(L) - (\max\{-\overline{tb}(L), -\overline{tb}(\overline{L})\} + 2) > M.$$

In fact, we can construct such a link as follows. Let $K = 8_9$. Then,

$$g(8_9) = 3 \text{ and } \max\{-\overline{tb}(8_9), -\overline{tb}(\overline{8_9})\} = 5.$$

Let K_n be the connected sum of n copies of 8_9, where we take the mirror image so that $\overline{tb}(8_9) = -5$. It is known that $\overline{tb}(K\sharp K') = \overline{tb}(K) + \overline{tb}(K') + 1$ for any knots K and K' [24]. Hence, we obtain

$$g(K_n) = 3n,$$
$$\overline{tb}(K_n) = n\overline{tb}(8_9) + (n-1) = -5n + n - 1 = -4n - 1.$$

By Theorem 1.2, we see that $6n + 2 \leq fpbk(K_n)$. Hence, we have

$$2fpbk(L) - (\max\{-\overline{tb}(L), -\overline{tb}(\overline{L})\} + 2) \geq 2(6n+2) - (4n+1+2) = 8n+1.$$

6.3 Front and Lagrangian Projections

For a Legendrian knot $\mathcal{L}$ in $\xi_{std} = \mathrm{Ker}(dz + xdy)$, the *front (or Lagrangian) projection* of $\mathcal{L}$ is the image $p(\mathcal{L})$ of $\mathcal{L}$ under the yz-projection map $p_{yz}\colon \mathbf{S}^3 = \mathbf{R}^3 \cup \{\infty\} \to \mathbf{R}^2$, which is given by $(x, y, z) \mapsto (y, z)$. Front projections are helpful to compute Thurston-Bennequin numbers and rotation numbers of the Legendrian links combinatorially.

So the following is a natural question: Find a method to draw a front projection of the Legendrian link $\mathcal{L}_F$ associated with a flat plumbing basket F. Fortunately, an answer to the question has been given in [12].

6.4 Tabulation

We improve [9, Table 1] as in Table 1, where we use Theorems 1.2, 1.3 and 1.4. In Table 1, $-\overline{tb}(K)$ means $\max\{-\overline{tb}(K), -\overline{tb}(\overline{K})\}$ and $-\overline{sl}(K)$ means $\max\{-\overline{sl}(K), -\overline{sl}(\overline{K})\}$. We refer to [18, Proposition 1.6] for $\overline{sl}(K)$ and [2] for $\overline{tb}(K)$. Note that $fpbk(K) \in 2\mathbf{Z}$ for a knot K.

In this table, the asterisks * are improved points of [9, Table 1]. The double asterisks ** are given by [3] and Mikami Hirasawa. In fact, Mikami Hirasawa taught the author that a flat basket code for 8_1 is $(1, 2, 4, 5, 3, 6, 1, 4, 6, 2, 5, 3)$ and a flat basket code for 9_{44} is $(1, 2, 5, 6, 1, 4, 3, 5, 6, 2, 4, 3)$. The daggers † mean that Theorem 1.3 or 1.4 detects $fpbk(K)$.

For example, 8_{15} has a flat plumbing basket presentation F with $b_1(F) = 10$. On the other hand, it is known that $\max\{-\overline{sl}(8_{15}), -\overline{sl}(\overline{8_{15}})\} = 11$ (see [18, Proposition 1.6]). Hence, by Theorem 1.3, we have $fpbk(8_{15}) = 10$.

For another example, the knot 9_{45} has a flat plumbing basket presentation F with $b_1(F) = 8$. On the other hand, it is known that $\max\{-\overline{tb}(9_{45}), -\overline{tb}(\overline{9_{45}})\} = 10$ (for example, see [2]). Moreover, 9_{45} is a non-torus knot. Hence, by Theorem 1.4, we have $10 + 3 = 13 \leq 2fpbk(9_{45}) \leq 16$. Since $fpbk(9_{45}) \in 2\mathbf{Z}$, we have $fpbk(9_{45}) = 8$.

Question 6.2. *Determine $fpbk(K)$ for $K = 9_{25}, 9_{34}, 9_{39}, 9_{40}, 9_{41}$ and 9_{43}.*

Note that $fpbk$ is subadditive under connected sum of knots. However, in general, it is not additive. For example, Hirose-Nakashima [9, Remark 1.4(b)] proved that $fpbk(3_1) = fpbk(\overline{3_1}) = 4$ but $fpbk(3_1\sharp\overline{3_1}) = 6$. Nao Kobayashi (Imoto) proved that $fpbk(6_1) = fpbk(\overline{6_1}) = 6$ but $fpbk(6_1\sharp\overline{6_1}) = 8$ in [15, Proposition 5.4].

Acknowledgements: The author was supported by JSPS KAKENHI Grant numbers JP16H07230 and JP18K13416.

Table 1: Table of flat plumbing basket numbers $fpbk(K)$ for prime knots K with up to 9 crossings. For the notations, see Section 6.4.

K	$-\overline{tb}(K)$	$-\overline{sl}(K)$	$fpbk(K)$	K	$-\overline{tb}(K)$	$-\overline{sl}(K)$	$fpbk(K)$
3_1	$6^\dagger$	$5^\dagger$	4	9_8	8	7	8
4_1	3	3	4	9_9	$16^\dagger$	$11^\dagger$	10
5_1	$10^\dagger$	$7^\dagger$	6	9_{10}	$14^\dagger$	$11^\dagger$	10^*
5_2	$8^\dagger$	$7^\dagger$	6	9_{11}	$12^\dagger$	$9^\dagger$	8
6_1	5	5	6	9_{12}	$10^\dagger$	$9^\dagger$	8
6_2	$7^\dagger$	5	6	9_{13}	$14^\dagger$	$11^\dagger$	10^*
6_3	4	3	6	9_{14}	7	7	8
7_1	$14^\dagger$	$9^\dagger$	8	9_{15}	$10^\dagger$	$9^\dagger$	8
7_2	$10^\dagger$	$9^\dagger$	8^*	9_{16}	$16^\dagger$	$11^\dagger$	10
7_3	$12^\dagger$	$9^\dagger$	8	9_{17}	8	5	8
7_4	$10^\dagger$	$9^\dagger$	8^*	9_{18}	$14^\dagger$	$11^\dagger$	10^*
7_5	$12^\dagger$	$9^\dagger$	8	9_{19}	6	5	8
7_6	$8^\dagger$	$7^\dagger$	6	9_{20}	$12^\dagger$	$9^\dagger$	8
7_7	5	5	6	9_{21}	$10^\dagger$	$9^\dagger$	8
8_1	$7^\dagger$	$7^\dagger$	6^{**}	9_{22}	8	5	8
8_2	$11^\dagger$	7	8	9_{23}	$14^\dagger$	$11^\dagger$	10^*
8_3	5	5	6	9_{24}	6	5	8
8_4	7	5	8	9_{25}	10	9	8–10
8_5	$11^\dagger$	7	8	9_{26}	9	7	8
8_6	9	7	8	9_{27}	6	5	8
8_7	8	5	8	9_{28}	9	7	8
8_8	6	5	8	9_{29}	8	5	8
8_9	5	3	8	9_{30}	6	5	8
8_{10}	8	5	8	9_{31}	9	7	8
8_{11}	9	7	8	9_{32}	9	7	8
8_{12}	5	5	6	9_{33}	6	5	8
8_{13}	6	5	8	9_{34}	6	5	8–12
8_{14}	9	7	8	9_{35}	12	$11^\dagger$	10^*
8_{15}	13	$11^\dagger$	10^*	9_{36}	$12^\dagger$	$9^\dagger$	8
8_{16}	8	5	8	9_{37}	6	5	8
8_{17}	5	3	8	9_{38}	$14^\dagger$	$11^\dagger$	10^*
8_{18}	5	3	8	9_{39}	10	9	8–10
8_{19}	12	$11^\dagger$	10^*	9_{40}	9	7	8–12
8_{20}	$6^\dagger$	5	6	9_{41}	7	7	8–10
8_{21}	$9^\dagger$	$7^\dagger$	6	9_{42}	5	5	6
9_1	$18^\dagger$	$11^\dagger$	10	9_{43}	10	9	8–10
9_2	12	$11^\dagger$	10^*	9_{44}	$6^\dagger$	5	6^{**}
9_3	$16^\dagger$	$11^\dagger$	10	9_{45}	$10^\dagger$	$9^\dagger$	8^*
9_4	$14^\dagger$	$11^\dagger$	10^*	9_{46}	$7^\dagger$	$7^\dagger$	6
9_5	12	$11^\dagger$	10^*	9_{47}	7	7	8
9_6	$16^\dagger$	$11^\dagger$	10	9_{48}	$8^\dagger$	$7^\dagger$	6
9_7	$14^\dagger$	$11^\dagger$	10^*	9_{49}	12	$11^\dagger$	10^*

References

[1] D. Bennequin, *Entrelacements et équations de Pfaff*, Third Schnepfenried geometry conference, Vol. 1 (Schnepfenried, 1982), Astérisque, vol. 107, Soc. Math. France, Paris, 1983, pp. 87–161. MR 753131 (86e:58070)

[2] J. C. Cha and C. Livingston, *KnotInfo*, http://www.indiana.edu/%7eknotinfo/.

[3] Y. H. Choi, Y. K. Chung, and D. Kim, *The complete list of prime knots whose flat plumbing basket numbers are 6 or less*, J. Knot Theory Ramifications **24** (2015), no. 7, 1550042, 13.

[4] J. B. Etnyre, L. L. Ng, and V. Vértesi, *Legendrian and transverse twist knots*, J. Eur. Math. Soc. (JEMS) **15** (2013), no. 3, 969–995. MR 3085098

[5] J. Franks and R. F. Williams, *Braids and the Jones polynomial*, Trans. Amer. Math. Soc. **303** (1987), no. 1, 97–108. MR 896009 (88k:57006)

[6] R. Furihata, M. Hirasawa, and T. Kobayashi, *Seifert surfaces in open books, and a new coding algorithm for links*, Bull. Lond. Math. Soc. **40** (2008), no. 3, 405–414. MR 2418796

[7] H. Geiges, *An introduction to contact topology*, Cambridge Studies in Advanced Mathematics, vol. 109, Cambridge University Press, Cambridge, 2008. MR 2397738

[8] E. Giroux, *Géométrie de contact: de la dimension trois vers les dimensions supérieures*, Proceedings of the International Congress of Mathematicians, Vol. II (Beijing, 2002), Higher Ed. Press, Beijing, 2002, pp. 405–414. MR 1957051

[9] S. Hirose and Y. Nakashima, *Seifert surfaces in open books, and pass moves on links*, J. Knot Theory Ramifications **23** (2014), no. 4, 1450021, 12. MR 3218929

[10] K. Honda, *On the classification of tight contact structures. I*, Geom. Topol. **4** (2000), 309–368. MR 1786111

[11] N. Imoto, *On an estimation of flat plumbing basket number of knots*, JP J. Geom. Topol. **18** (2015), no. 1, 65–84. MR 3445276

[12] T. Ito and K. Tagami, *Flat plumbing basket and contact structure*, J. Knot Theory Ramifications **30** (2021), no. 2, Paper No. 2150010, 17. MR 4244976

[13] D. Kim, *An alternating labeling on a spanning tree of seifert graphs and applications in knot theory*, arXiv:1108.1455.

[14] D. Kim, Y. S. Kwon, and J. Lee, *Banded surfaces, banded links, band indices and genera of links*, J. Knot Theory Ramifications **22** (2013), no. 7, 1350035, 18. MR 3084753

[15] N. Kobayashi (Imoto), *Basket diagram and its application to flat plumbing basket number of links*, 2017, Thesis (Ph.D.)–Nara Women's University.

[16] H. R. Morton, *Seifert circles and knot polynomials*, Math. Proc. Cambridge Philos. Soc. **99** (1986), no. 1, 107–109. MR 809504 (87c:57006)

[17] L. Ng, *A Legendrian Thurston-Bennequin bound from Khovanov homology*, Algebr. Geom. Topol. **5** (2005), 1637–1653. MR 2186113

[18] ———, *On arc index and maximal Thurston-Bennequin number*, J. Knot Theory Ramifications **21** (2012), no. 4, 1250031, 11. MR 2890458

[19] B. Ozbagci and A. I. Stipsicz, *Surgery on contact 3-manifolds and Stein surfaces*, Bolyai Society Mathematical Studies, vol. 13, Springer-Verlag, Berlin; János Bolyai Mathematical Society, Budapest, 2004. MR 2114165

[20] O. Plamenevskaya, *Transverse knots and Khovanov homology*, Math. Res. Lett. **13** (2006), no. 4, 571–586. MR 2250492 (2007d:57043)

[21] A. N. Shumakovitch, *Rasmussen invariant, slice-Bennequin inequality, and sliceness of knots*, J. Knot Theory Ramifications **16** (2007), no. 10, 1403–1412. MR 2384833 (2008m:57034)

[22] T. Tanaka, *Maximal Bennequin numbers and Kauffman polynomials of positive links*, Proc. Amer. Math. Soc. **127** (1999), no. 11, 3427–3432. MR 1616601

[23] W. Thurston and H. Winkelnkemper, *On the existence of contact forms*, Proc. Amer. Math. Soc. **52** (1975), 345–347. MR 0375366

[24] I. Torisu, *On the additivity of the Thurston-Bennequin invariant of Legendrian knots*, Pacific J. Math. **210** (2003), no. 2, 359–365. MR 1988540

Chapter 6

Improving Speciation-Based Particle Swarm Optimization with Graphs by Sphere Mutation, Local Mutation, and Parameter Adjustment for Multimodal Optimization

Setsuko Sakai* and Tetsuyuki Takahama**
*Faculty of Commercial Sciences, Hiroshima Shudo University
1-1 Ozuka-Higashi 1-chome, Asaminami-ku, Hiroshima, JAPAN 731-3195
**Graduate School of Information Sciences, Hiroshima City University
4-1 Ozuka-Higashi 3-chome, Asaminami-ku, Hiroshima, JAPAN 731-3194

Abstract

Multimodal optimization is a very difficult task to search for all optimal solutions at once in optimization problems with multiple optimal solutions. Speciation using proximity graphs has been studied as a method for solving multimodal optimization problems. It has been shown that speciation-based particle swarm optimization with β-relaxed relative neighborhood graph (SPSO-G/βRNG) can search for many optimal solutions with high accuracy. In multimodal optimization, search points are divided into some species and each species searches a different region, so it is necessary to enhance the local search ability. In this study, we propose three methods to improve SPSO-G/βRNG by enhancing the local search ability: introducing sphere mutation, introducing local mutation, and adjusting PSO parameters. In sphere mutation, in order to search the immediate vicinity of a candidate of optimal solutions, a random search is performed within the hypersphere whose center is the candidate and whose radius is the distance to the nearest search point. In local mutation, a mutation operation in differential evolution (DE) is used, where the difference vector is selected from neighbor search points rather than from all search points. In the PSO parameter adjustment, a large value of cognitive parameter and a small value of social parameter are adopted. The performance of the proposed method is shown by optimizing well-known benchmark problems for "CEC'2013 special session and competition on niching methods for multimodal function optimization".

Key Words:

multimodal optimization, particle swarm optimization, graph-based speciation, proximity graph

1. Introduction

There exist many studies on solving optimization problems using population-based optimization algorithms (POAs) in which a population or multiple search points are used to search for an optimal solution. Swarm intelligence algorithms inspired by collective animal behavior such as particle swarm optimization (PSO) [1] and ant colony optimization are POAs. In general, POAs are stochastic direct search methods, which only need function values to be optimized, and are easy to implement. For this reason, POAs have been successfully applied to various optimization problems.

In some optimization problems, it is sometimes desirable to find as many optimal solutions as possible including suboptimal solutions instead of finding only one optimal solution. For example, in industrial design problems, due to the presence of manufacturing errors, solutions whose function values vary rapidly in the neighborhood of the solutions are undesireble. It is good idea that a solution is selected from perspectives such as the stability of the solution in the neighborhood after finding as many solutions as possible. An optimization problem with multiple optimal solutions is called multimodal optimization problem (MMOP). When trying to solve the MMOPs with POAs, the diversity of search points decreases as the search progresses generally and the search points converge near a certain solution. Therefore, MMOPs are very difficult to solve and researches on MMOPs are actively conducted to find multiple solutions in one trial.

In order to obtain multiple solutions, it is required that the search points are divided into several subpopulations, each subpopulation is responsible for a different search subspace, and the search is performed by each subpopulation with maintaining diversity. This technique is called niching or speciation [2, 3]. Representative methods include: sharing, clearing, crowding, speciation according to the radius of the subpopulation [4, 5], speciation using a clustering method [6], and speciation using a proximity graph [7, 8].

We have been studying multimodal optimization using speciation-based PSO with graphs (SPSO-G). In [9], we proposed β-relaxed RNG (βRNG) which can realize an intermediate graph between Gabriel Graph (GG) and Relative Neighborhood Graph (RNG) by changing β. By reducing β from 2 to 1, sufficient number of species are formed by sparse graphs like RNG initially in order not to miss optimal solutions, and then the number of species are gradually reduced to find precise solutions by dense graphs like GG. As for the PSO parameters, the inertia weight was set to 0.4 to emphasize local search ability for the seeds, which are the best particles in the species, and particles adjacent to the seeds. For other particles, the inertia weight was set to a uniform random number in [0.4, 0.9] to emphasize global search ability. Also, the species-best mutation operation, which is similar to the DE/best/1/bin operation in differential evolution (DE), is adopted where the base vector is not the best search point but the species-best point. The total mean peak rate for CEC2013 benchmark problems was 0.833054. In [10], we proposed a crossover operation with an adaptive crossover rate to improve the search accuracy of functions with a large number of optimal solutions and a regular distribution of optimal solutions, such as the three-dimensional Vincent function. In the crossover operation, candidates for optimal solutions are selected by hill-valley detection method, and a new solution is generated by randomly combining elements of the candidates. The total mean peak rate for CEC2013 benchmark problems improved to 0.841589.

In this study, we propose three methods to improve SPSO-G/βRNG by enhancing the local search ability: introducing sphere mutation, introducing local mutation, and adjusting PSO parameters. In sphere mutation, in order to search the immediate vicinity of a candidate of optimal solutions, the hypersphere whose center is the candidate and whose radius is the distance to the nearest search point is formed, and a new solution is generated randomly and uniformly in the hypersphere. In local mutation, a mutation operation in differential evolution (DE) is used, where the difference vector is selected from search points in the neighborhood of the parent rather than from all search points. As the vector becomes smaller, the search range becomes narrower, and the local search can be realized. In PSO parameter adjustment, the cognitive parameter which controls the weight of search around each search point is increased and the social parameter which controls the weight of search around the seed is decreased. The performance of the proposed method is shown by optimizing well-known benchmark problems for "CEC'2013 special session and competition on niching methods for multimodal function optimization" [11].

In Section 2, proximity graphs and βRNG are explained. Speciation methods are explained in Section 3. In Section 4, PSO and SPSO-G/βRNG is briefly explained. Two mutation operations and the PSO parameter adjustment are proposed in Section 5. The experimental results are shown in Section 6. Finally, conclusions are described in Section 7.

2. Proximity Graphs

2.1 Definition

Graph G can be described $G(V, E)$ where V is the set of vertices and E is the set of edges. A proximity graph is a graph in which two vertices are connected by an edge if and only if the vertices satisfy particular geometric requirements. When two vertices $v_i, v_j \in V$ satisfy a neighborhood condition, the vertices have an edge $(v_i, v_j) \in E$. Nearest neighborhood graph, Gabriel graph [12], relative neighborhood graph [13], β skeleton [14] are proposed as proximity graphs.

In Gabriel graph (GG), two vertices v_i and v_j satisfy the neighborhood condition when the hypersphere, of which diameter is the line between the vertices, does not have any other vertex inside of the hypersphere. GG can be defined as follows:

$$(v_i, v_j) \in E \iff HS\left(\frac{v_i + v_j}{2}, \frac{||v_i - v_j||}{2}\right) \cap V = \phi \tag{1}$$

where $HS(\boldsymbol{c}, r)$ shows the hypersphere with radius r centered at $\boldsymbol{c}$.

$$HS(\boldsymbol{c}, r) = \{\boldsymbol{x} \,|\, ||\boldsymbol{x} - \boldsymbol{c}|| < r\} \tag{2}$$

If and only if any vertex v_k does not exists in the hypersphere, the vertices are connected by an edge.

In relative neighborhood graph (RNG), two vertices v_i and v_j satisfy the neighborhood condition when the intersection of two hyperspheres with radius $||v_i - v_j||$ centered at v_i and v_j does not have any other vertices inside of the intersection. The intersection is called as a lune.

RNG can be defined as follows:

$$(v_i, v_j) \in E \iff HS(v_i, ||v_i - v_j||) \cap \tag{3}$$
$$HS(v_j, ||v_i - v_j||) \cap V = \phi$$

RNG is a subgraph of GG.

2.2 β-relaxed Relative Neighborhood Graph

We proposed a new proximity graph with a parameter β named β-relaxed RNG (βRNG) [9]. The neighborhood condition for βRNG is that no other vertices are included in the intersection of the RNG lune and the hypersphere specified by the parameter β. For a pair of vertices v_i and v_j, a hypersphere centered at the midpoint of the two vertices is defined so that a point $\boldsymbol{u}$ on the hypersphere satisfies the following equation:

$$\beta = \frac{||v_i - \boldsymbol{u}||^2 + ||v_j - \boldsymbol{u}||^2}{||v_i - v_j||^2}, \ 1 \le \beta \le 2 \tag{4}$$

This can be transformed as follows:

$$||\boldsymbol{u} - \frac{v_i + v_j}{2}||^2 = \left(\frac{\sqrt{2\beta - 1}}{2}||v_i - v_j||\right)^2 \tag{5}$$

Therefore, βRNG(V, E) can be defined as follows:

$$(v_i, v_j) \in E \iff \tag{6}$$
$$HS(v_i, ||v_i - v_j||) \cap HS(v_j, ||v_i - v_j||) \cap$$
$$HS\left(\frac{v_i + v_j}{2}, \frac{\sqrt{2\beta - 1}}{2}||v_i - v_j||\right) \cap V = \phi$$

Figure 1 shows an example of βRNG, where the shaded region is the conditional region when β=1.5. βRNG is a subgraph of GG and a supergraph of RNG. Similar to the β skeleton, βRNG of β=1 is GG and βRNG of β=2 is RNG.

The neighborhood condition of two vertices in βRNG can be determined as follows:

- If there exists no vertex v_k which satisfies $||v_i - v_k|| < ||v_i - v_j||$, $||v_j - v_k|| < ||v_i - v_j||$ and $||v_i - v_k||^2 + ||v_j - v_k||^2 < \beta ||v_i - v_j||^2$, v_i and v_j is connected.

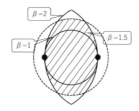

Figure 1. Neighborhood condition for βRNG when $\beta = 1.5$

3. Speciation

Speciation is biologically an evolutionary process to form new biological species by the development of one species into two or more genetically distinct ones. The idea of speciation has been mainly used for multimodal optimization to capture multiple optimal or suboptimal solutions simultaneously. Each species evolves to find an optimal or a suboptimal solution.

There exist some types of speciation methods [15] such as radius-based speciation, nearest neighbor-based speciation and graph-based speciation. In the following, a population of search points, or individuals is described as $P = \{x_i \,|\, i = 1, 2, \cdots, N\}$ where N is the population size and P is the target of speciation. The seed of a species to which an individual x_i belongs is denoted by $x_{seed(x_i)}$.

3.1 Radius-Based Speciation

In radius-based speciation, the neighborhood condition is defined by species radius R [5, 16, 17]. A species is composed of a species seed and individuals inside the hypersphere of radius R centered at the seed. Given individuals and an objective value for each individual, the algorithm for radius-based speciation is described as follows:

1. A population is sorted according to the objective values in the order of best objective value first.

2. The best individual x_b in the sorted population becomes a new species seed ($seed(x_b) = b$). The population members that exist within the specified radius from the seed are assigned to the species ($seed(x_i) = b$).

3. The members of the species including the seed are deleted from the population.

4. Go back to 2 until the population becomes empty.

In this speciation, it is difficult to select a proper radius, which depends on problems to be optimization and also the search process in the optimization.

3.2 Graph-Based Speciation

In graph-based speciation, a species is composed of an individual and its adjacent individuals that are connected to the individual by edges in a graph. In radius-based speciation, a species is formed by the best individual and the individuals within the species radius, where both individuals are selected from individuals whose species has not been determined. Similarly, in graph-based speciation, a species can be formed by the best individual and the individuals adjacent to the best individual. In this case, for example, if the second best individual is adjacent to the best individual, the second best individual cannot become a seed. In this study, the following speciation is adopted in order to avoid such situation.

1. A proximity graph is generated and the set of edges E is determined.

2. For each individual $x_i, i = 1, 2, \cdots, N$,

   (1) The adjacent individuals of x_i are obtained using E. A group is composed of x_i and the adjacent individuals.

   (2) The best individual in the group is the seed of x_i. In case of function maximization, the seed can be defined as follows:

$$seed(x_i) = \arg\max_{h \in H} f(x_h), \tag{7}$$
$$H = \{h | h = i \text{ or } (x_i, x_h) \in E\}$$

   where $seed(\cdot)$ returns the id of the seed. The seed of x_i is denoted by $x_{seed(x_i)}$.

3. Individuals with the same seed form a species.

   The list of all seeds is defined by $\{x_i \mid seed(x_i) = i\}$.

4. Multimodal Optimization Using SPSO-G/βRNG

4.1 Optimization Problems

An function maximization problem with lower bound and upper bound constraints can be described as follows:

$$\begin{aligned} \text{maximize} \quad & f(x) \\ \text{subject to} \quad & l_i \leq x_i \leq u_i, \; i = 1, \ldots, D, \end{aligned} \tag{8}$$

where $x = (x_1, x_2, \cdots, x_D)$ is a D dimensional vector and $f(x)$ is an objective function. The function f is a nonlinear real-valued function. Values l_i and u_i are the lower bound and the upper bound of x_i, respectively. The region that satisfies the upper and lower bound constraints is called search space.

4.2 Particle Swarm Optimization

PSO [1, 18] is an optimization method based on swarm intelligence which is inspired by the movement of a bird flock. PSO imitates the movement to solve optimization problems and is considered as a population-based stochastic search method or POA.

Searching procedures by PSO can be described as follows: A group of agents optimizes the objective function f. At any time t, each agent i knows its current position $\boldsymbol{x}_i^t$ and velocity $\boldsymbol{v}_i^t$ ($i = 1, 2, \cdots, N$). It also remembers its personal best visited position found so far $\boldsymbol{x}_i^*$ and the objective value $pbest_i$.

$$\boldsymbol{x}_i^{*t} = \arg\max_{\tau=0,1,\cdots,t} f(\boldsymbol{x}_i^\tau), \; pbest_i = f(\boldsymbol{x}_i^{*t}) \tag{9}$$

Two models, gbest model and lbest model have been proposed [19, 20]. In the gbest model, every agent knows the best visited position $\boldsymbol{x}_G^*$ in all agents and its objective value $gbest$. In the lbest model, each agent knows the best visited position $\boldsymbol{x}_l^*$ in the neighbors and its objective value $lbest_i$ as follows, where the neighbors are defined by a topology such as ring, mesh, star and tree topology.

$$\boldsymbol{x}_l^{*t} = \arg\max_{k \in N_i} f(\boldsymbol{x}_k^{*t}), \; lbest_i = f(\boldsymbol{x}_l^{*t}) \tag{10}$$

where N_i is the set of neighbor agents to i. In the gbest model, $l = G$, N_i is all agents and $lbest_i$ is $gbest$. The velocity of the agent i at time $t+1$ is defined as follows:

$$v_{ij}^{t+1} = w v_{ij}^t + c_1 \, rand_{1ij} \, (x_{ij}^{*t} - x_{ij}^t) \tag{11}$$
$$+ c_2 \, rand_{2ij} \, (x_{lj}^{*t} - x_{ij}^t)$$

where w is an inertia weight and $rand_{kij}$ is a uniform random number in $[0, 1]$ which is generated in each dimension. c_1 is a cognitive parameter and c_2 is a social parameter which represent the weight of the movement to the personal best position and the group/neighbors best position, respectively. Usually, the maximum velocity $V_j^{\max}$ is specified to avoid too large velocity and $|v_{ij}| \leq V_j^{\max}$ is satisfied.

The position of the agent i at time $t+1$ is given as follows:

$$\boldsymbol{x}_i^{t+1} = \boldsymbol{x}_i^t + \boldsymbol{v}_i^{t+1} \tag{12}$$

The linearly decreasing inertia weight (LDIW) method [21] is one of well-known strategies, where w is linearly decreasing with the number of iterations as follows:

$$w = w_{\max} - (w_{\max} - w_{\min}) \frac{t}{T_{\max}} \tag{13}$$

where $w_{\max}$ and $w_{\min}$ are the maximum weight and the minimum weight for w, respectively. $T_{\max}$ is the maximum number of iterations. Recommended values are $w_{\max}$=0.9, $w_{\min}$=0.4, $c_1=c_2$=2 and $V_j^{\max}=u_j$.

Also, several methods for inertia weight have been studied [22].

4.3 SPSO-G/βRNG

In SPSO-G/βRNG, graph-based speciation using "personal best positions", or $P=\{x_i^*\}$ is adopted because the personal best positions have more accurate information about local optimal solutions than particle positions.

The following modifications to standard PSO are applied for SPSO-G/βRNG:

- If an edge is too long, it is likely to connect vertices belonging to different species. Edges that satisfy the following equation are removed in order to cut about 10% long edges.

$$d > \bar{d} + 1.281552\sigma \qquad (14)$$

where d is the length of an edge, and $\bar{d}$ and σ are average and standard deviation of all lengths of edges, respectively.

- The proximity graph βRNG is used for speciation. The parameter β is dynamically changed according to the number of iterations where the β is linearly decreasing from 2 (RNG) to 1 (GG).

- If $seed(x_i^*) = i$, x_i^* is the best position in a species and is a candidate of an optimal solution. Also, if $seed(x_i^*) = l$ and $seed(x_l^*) = l$, x_i^* is adjacent to the candidate. In these cases, the inertia weight w is 0.4 in order to search in a small area near the candidate. In other cases, the inertia weight w is $0.5 + 0.4u(0,1)$ in order to search in wide areas, where $u(a,b)$ is a uniform random number in $[a,b]$.

- Species-best mutation [23] is adopted as follows:

$$m_i^t = x_{seed(x_i^{*t})}^{*t} + F(x_{r2}^{*t} - x_{r3}^{*t}) \qquad (15)$$

$$x_{ij}^{t+1} = \begin{cases} m_{ij}^t, & \text{if } j = j_{rand} \text{ or } u(0,1) < CR \\ x_{ij}^{*t}, & otherwise \end{cases} \qquad (16)$$

$$v_{ij}^{t+1} = u(0,1)(x_{ij}^{*t} - x_{ij}^{t+1}) \qquad (17)$$

where r_2 and r_3 are random numbers in $\{1, 2, \cdots, N\}$ excluding i and are different from each other, F is a scaling factor, j_{rand} is a randomly selected integer in $[1, D]$ (D is the number of dimensions), and CR is a crossover rate. The velocity is reset to a randomized direction from x_i^{t+1} to the personal best position. The mutation is applied with probability $P_m = 0.2$ with $F=1$ and $CR=0.1$.

- When a new position is out of the search space, the position is repaired to be the upper or lower bound. Also, the velocity is changed to $-\frac{1}{2}v_{ij}^{t+1}$ so that the bounds are not violated again.

- An archive is adopted to hold many solutions. The archive is initially filled by initial particle positions. When an particle moved and the new position is generated, the new position is stored if the number of the solutions in the archive is less than the archive size N_A. Otherwise the position is checked whether it may be stored in the archive or not. If the position is better than the closest solution in the archive, the closest solution is replaced with the new position.

4.4 The Crossover Operation with an Adaptive Crossover Rate

In the crossover operation, hill-valley detection and adaptive control of the crossover rate were proposed.

4.4.1 Hill-Valley detection

After a proximity graph is created, for each point x_i^* all edges $(x_i^*, x_j^*) \in E$ are checked. A point x_i^* is a valley point, if there exist one or more than one points in $\{x_j^*\}$ which have larger function values than x_i^* and there exist no point in $\{x_j^*\}$ which has smaller function value. A point x_i^* is a hill point, if there exist one or more than one points in $\{x_j^*\}$ with smaller function values and there exist no point in $\{x_j^*\}$ with larger function value.

4.4.2 The Crossover Operation

Let hill points be denoted by H because maximization is considered. It is assumed that the crossover operation is applied to an particle x_i^t and x_i^{t+1} is generated. The multi-parents crossover is explained because the crossover was better than two-parents crossover:

- For each j-th element of x_i^{t+1},

(1) A parent p is randomly selected from H.

(2) The element value is set to the j-th element of p.

The j-th element of the velocity v_{ij}^{t+1} is updated as a random value in $[-V_j^{\max}, V_j^{\max}]$.

4.4.3 Adaptive Control of Crossover Rate

The crossover operations are effective to functions whose optimal solutions are regularly distributed. However, for other functions, the crossover would result in a useless search and the search efficiency would decrease. We proposed to introduce a crossover rate and control it adaptively.

The algorithm of adaptive control of crossover rate is as follows:

1. Crossover rate P_c is initialized. Recommended value is 0.05.

2. The number of times crossover is performed T_c=0, and the number of times the crossover is successful S_c=0 where the new position generated by the crossover is better than the personal best position.

3. For each iteration and each particle, the crossover is selected with probability P_c.

4. If the crossover is selected, the crossover is applied to an particle, a new position is generated, and T_c is incremented by 1.

5. If the new position is better than the personal best position, S_c is incremented by 1.

6. After one iteration, the success rate of the crossover is calculated by $sr = \frac{S_c}{T_c}$.

7. If $sr \geq 0.7$, P_c is increased by 0.01. If $sr \leq 0.5$, P_c is decreased by 0.01. If $P_c > 0.1$, $P_c = 0.1$.

5. Proposed Method

Two mutation operations and parameter adjustment are proposed in this section. Modifications from original SPSO-G/βRNG are also explained.

5.1 Mutation Operations

Sphere Mutation If a personal best position x_i^* is a seed, in order to prevent the particle from leaving the current species, the new position is randomly generated within a hypersphere whose center is x_i^* and whose radius is the distance to the nearest personal best position as follows:

$$r_j \sim N(0,1), \ j = 1, 2, \cdots, D \tag{18}$$

$$x_{ij}^{t+1} = x_{ij}^* + \frac{r_j \sqrt[D]{u(0,1)}}{\sqrt{\sum_{j=1}^{D} r_j^2}} d_{\min} \tag{19}$$

$$v_i = 0 \tag{20}$$

where $N(0,1)$ is a normal distribution with the mean 0 and the standard deviation 1 and $d_{\min}$ is the distance between x_i^* and the nearest best position x_j^*, $j \neq i$. The velocity is set to the zero vector.

Local Mutation In DE, a difference vector $x_{r2} - x_{r3}$ is selected from a population, or all personal best positions in PSO. In this study, we refer to this type of mutation as global mutation. In the global mutation, the difference vector is often obtained from different species, so the difference vector is often large, making it difficult to realize local search such as searching around the species. For this reason, in the local mutation, the difference vector is taken from the NS nearest neighbor personal best positions to limit the search range, where NS is the neighborhood size and $NS=9$. Since both the global mutation and the local mutation are required, both mutation operations are performed with probability $0.5P_m$ where P_m is mutation probability and $P_m=0.3$. As for parameter values, $F = 0.5$ and $CR = 0.2$ in the global mutation, and F is a uniform random value in $[0.4, 1]$ and $CR = 0.9$ in the local mutation. Also, the velocity update rule for the species-best mutation, Eq.(17) is changed as follows:

$$v_i^{t+1} = x_i^{t+1} - x_i^t \tag{21}$$

5.2 Other Modifications

Some other modifications from SPSO-G/βRNG with adaptive crossover are introduced.

- The processing when a personal best position is the seed and when it is adjacent to the seed is separated. When it is the seed, the sphere mutation is applied to the particle. When it is adjacent, the particle moves as in SPSO-G/βRNG.

- In the crossover, the velocity is updated to the zero vector instead of a random number in $[-V_j^{\max}, V_j^{\max}]$.

- In order to increase the number of candidates, all seeds are used instead of hill points, so hill-valley detection is not used. Therefore, the list of all seeds is used for H in the crossover operation.

- The PSO parameter c_1 is adjusted as 3 to enhance local search around each particle and c_2 is adjusted as 1 to weaken the convergence to the seed.

5.3 Algorithm

The algorithm of proposed method, improved SPSO-G/βRNG is as follows:

1. The number of particles N and the archive size N_A are specified. Usually, $N_A = N$.

2. Initialization: Initial particles $\{i \mid i = 1, 2, \cdots, N\}$ with a position x_i and a velocity v_i are generated. x_i is randomly generated in the search space where each element x_{ij} is a uniform random number in $[l_j, u_j]$. $v_i = \mathbf{0}$ and $V_j^{\max} = \frac{1}{2}(u_j - l_j)$. $x_i^* = x_i$. The archive is filled by the initial particle positions. P_c is initialized to 0.05.

3. Termination: If the number of function evaluations exceeds the maximum number of function evaluations $FE_{\max}$, the algorithm is terminated.

4. Speciation: For dynamic control of graph, β is updated as $\beta = 2 - \frac{FE}{FE_{\max}}$ where FE is the current number of function evaluations. βRNG is created using $\{x_i^*\}$. Long edges are removed according to Eq.(14). $seed(x_i^*)$ is determined according to the graph-based speciation algorithm. The list of all seeds is obtained as $S = \{x_i \mid seed(x_i) = i\}$.

5. Update of particles: Mainly, the particles are updated by the movement. If x_i^* is a seed, or $seed(x_i^*) = i$, the sphere mutation is applied. If it is adjacent to a seed, or $seed(x_{seed(x_i^*)}^*)$

= $seed(x_i^*)$, PSO parameters $(w, c_1, c_2) = (0.4, 2, 2)$. Otherwise $(w, c_1, c_2) = (0.5 + 0.4u(0,1), 3, 1)$. The new velocity of each particle i are obtained according to Eq.(11). Each element of the new velocity is truncated in $[-V_{max_j}, V_{max_j}]$. The new position is obtained according to Eq.(12). When x_i is not near the seed, the position is updated by the crossover using S with probability P_c if the dimension of the problem is greater than 1 and the number of seeds in S is greater than the dimension. Also, the global mutation and the local mutation is applied to the particle with probability $0.5 P_m$ where P_m=0.3. If the position is out of the search space, the position and the velocity is repaired.

6. Update of personal best: If the objective value of the new position $f(x_i^{t+1})$ is better than that of the personal best position $f(x_i^*)$, the personal best position is replaced with the new position.

7. Update of the archive: The archive is updated by newly generated positions.

8. Adaptive control of the crossover rate P_c: If $T_c > 1$, P_c is updated according to the algorithm described in Section 4.4.3.

9. Go back to 3.

Figure 2 show the algorithm of the proposed method improved SPSO-G/βRNG. The lines starting with '+' show the modified lines from SPSO/βRNG with adaptive crossover.

6. Numerical Experiments

6.1 Test Problems and performance evaluation

In this study, the benchmark problems for "CEC'2013 special session and competition on niching methods for multimodal function optimization" are optimized. Brief explanation of 20 benchmark problems are shown in Table 1. The problem number (Prob.), the function name with the number of dimensions, the optimal value, the number of global optima, and function description are described for each problem.

In order to evaluate the performance, the following measures are used [11]:

Peak ratio (PR): Given a maximum number of function evaluations and an accuracy level, PR measures the average ratio of all known global optima found in all runs. If all global optima are found in all runs, PR is 1.

$$PR = \frac{\sum_{i=1}^{NR} NPF_i}{NKP * NR} \quad (22)$$

where NR is the number of runs, NPF_i is the number of global optima found in the end of i-th run, NKP is the number of known global optima. When the difference between the best objective value found and the global optimal value is less than or equal to the accuracy level, it is considered

Improving PSO with Graph-based Speciation for Multimodal Optimization 93

```
   Initialize particles P={(x_i, v_i)|i = 1, 2, ···, N};
   x_i^* = x_i, i=1, 2, ···, N;
   for(each dimension j)  V_j^max = 1/2 (u_j − l_j);
   P_c=0.05;
   FE=N; // number of function evaluations
   for(each x_i in P) UpdateArchive(x_i, A);
   for(t=1; FE < FE_max; t++) {
     Update β;
     Create βRNG using {x_i^* | i = 1, 2, ···, N};
     Cut long edges whose length is greater than d̄ + 1.281552σ;
     Graph-based speciation using the βRNG to obtain seed(x_i^*);
+    S=list of all seeds;
     T_c=S_c=0;
     for(each particle i in P) {
        crossflag=0;
        l=seed(x_i^*);
+       if(l == i) {
+          x_i=generated by the sphere mutation; goto Eval;
+       }
+       else if(seed(x_l^*) == l)  w=0.4, c_1 = c_2 = 2;
+       else if(D>1 && |S| ≥ D && u(0,1)<P_c) { // crossover
+          x_i=generated by the multi-parent crossover using S; v_i=0;
          T_c+=1; crossflag=1; goto Eval:
        }
        else if(u(0,1)<Pm) { // mutation
+          x_i^old=x_i;
+          if(u(0,1)<0.5) x_i=generated by the global mutation;
+          else x_i=generated by the local mutation;
+          v_i=x_i − x_i^old; goto Eval;
        }
        else
+          w=0.5+0.4u(0,1), c_1 = 3, c_2 = 1;
        for(each dimension j) {
          v_ij=wv_ij+c_1 rand_1ij (x_ij^* − x_ij)+c_2 rand_2ij (x_lj^* − x_ij);
          if(v_ij>V_j^max)  v_ij=V_j^max; else if(v_ij<−V_j^max)  v_ij=−V_j^max;
          x_ij=x_ij+v_ij;
        }
     Eval:
        for(each dimension j)
           if(x_ij<l_j)  x_ij=l_j, v_ij=−1/2v_ij; else if(x_ij>u_j)  x_ij=u_j, v_ij=−1/2v_ij;
        if(f(x_i) > f(x_i^*)) {
           x_i^*=x_i;
           if(crossflag) S_c+=1;
        }
        UpdateArchive(x_i, A);
        FE=FE+1;
        if(FE>=FE_max) break;
     }
     if(T_c>0) { // adaptive control of P_c
        sr=S_c/T_c;
        if(sr ≥0.7)  P_c+=0.01; else if(sr ≤0.5)  P_c−=0.01;
        if(P_c>0.1)  P_c=0.1;
     }
   }
   return A as the optimal solution candidates

UpdateArchive(x, A) {
  if(|A|<N_A)  A=A ∪ {x};
  else {
     x_nn=arg min_{x_a ∈ A} ||x_a − x||;
     if(f(x) ≥ f(x_nn))  x_nn=x;
  }
}
```

Figure 2. Algorithm of improved SPSO-G/βRNG

Table 1. Benchmark functions

Prob.	Function	Optimal value	#global optima	Function description
1	F_1 (1D)	200.0	2	Five-Uneven-Peak Trap
2	F_2 (1D)	1.0	5	Equal Maxima
3	F_3 (1D)	1.0	1	Uneven Decreasing Maxima
4	F_4 (2D)	200.0	4	Himmelblau
5	F_5 (2D)	1.03163	2	Six-Hump Camel Back
6	F_6 (2D)	186.731	18	Shubert (2D)
7	F_7 (2D)	1.0	36	Vincent (2D)
8	F_6 (3D)	2709.0935	81	Shubert (3D)
9	F_7 (3D)	1.0	216	Vincent (3D)
10	F_8 (2D)	-2.0	12	Modified Rastrigin - All Global Optima
11	F_9 (2D)	0	6	Composition Function 1
12	F_{10} (2D)	0	8	Composition Function 2
13	F_{11} (2D)	0	6	Composition Function 3 (2D)
14	F_{11} (3D)	0	6	Composition Function 3 (3D)
15	F_{12} (3D)	0	8	Composition Function 4 (3D)
16	F_{11} (5D)	0	6	Composition Function 3 (5D)
17	F_{12} (5D)	0	8	Composition Function 4 (5D)
18	F_{11} (10D)	0	6	Composition Function 3 (10D)
19	F_{12} (10D)	0	8	Composition Function 4 (10D)
20	F_{12} (20D)	0	8	Composition Function 4 (20D)

to have found a global optimal solution. Five accuracy levels 1e-1, 1e-2, 1e-3, 1e-4 and 1e-5 are adopted.

6.2 Experimental Conditions

The 20 benchmark problems are optimized by improved SPSO-G/βRNG. In order to investigate the effect of the improvements, improved SPSO-G/βRNG without the sphere mutation (NoSM), without the local mutation (NoLM), and without parameter adjustment (NoPar) are tested. In NoSM, when a personal best is a seed or adjacent to the seed, PSO movement with w=0.4 is adopted as original SPSO-G/βRNG. In NoLM, the local mutation is not adopted and the global mutation is executed with probability P_m as original SPSO-G/βRNG. In NoPar, c_1=c_2=2.

The maximum numbers of function evaluations are specified for each function: 5.0e+04 in F_1 to F_5 (1D or 2D), 2.0e+05 in F_6 to F_{11} (2D), and 4.0e+05 in F_6 to F_{12} (3D or higher).

The population sizes are specified for each problem: N=50 in problems 1, 2, 3, 4, 5 and 10, N=150 in problem 6, N=400 in problems 8, 18, 19 and 20, N=750 in problem 7, N=1500 in problem 9, and N=300 in the other problems. The archive size N_A=N. For each problem, 50 runs are performed.

6.3 Experimental Results

Tables 2 and 3 show the experimental results. The first column shows the problem number. The third column labeled ϵ shows the accuracy levels. The columns labeled NMMSO, Imp.SPSO-G/βRNG, NoSM, NoLM and NoPar show a PR value for each accuracy level and the mean PR value for all accuracy levels over 50 runs in case of NMMSO (Niching Migratory Multi-Swarm Optimiser) [24], improved SPSO-G/βRNG, improved SPSO-G/βRNG without the sphere mutation, improved SPSO-G/βRNG without the local mutation, and improved SPSO-G/βRNG without the parameter adjustment, respectively. NMMSO is a very good PSO-based multimodal optimization algorithm and ranked first in the CEC competition on Niching Methods for Multimodal Optimization in 2015 and 2017. Best mean PR values among all methods are highlighted in bold.

Improved SPSO-G/βRNG attained the best mean PR values in seven problems 6, 10, 11, 14, 16, 17 and 20. Improved SPSO-G/βRNG without the sphere mutation attained the best mean PR values in problem 6. Improved SPSO-G/βRNG without the local mutation attained the best mean PR values in four problems 6, 8, 18 and 19. Improved SPSO-G/βRNG without parameter adjustment attained the best mean PR values in five problems 6, 9, 15 and 18. NMMSO attained the best mean PR values in four functions 7, 10, 12 and 13. In terms of the number of functions that achieved the best PR value, improved SPSO-G/βRNG attained the best result.

NMMSO achieved 0.8221 as the total mean PR value for all accuracy levels and all problems. Improved SPSO-G/βRNG, improved SPSO-G/βRNG without the sphere mutation, Improved SPSO-G/βRNG without the local mutation and Improved SPSO-G/βRNG without the parameter adjustment achieved 0.856195, 0.836673, 0.850768 and 0.8523220 as the total mean PR values, respectively, which are better results than NMMSO. It is thought that the effect of the sphere mutation is large and the effect of the local mutation and the parameter adjustment is small.

The latest competitions based on the CEC2013 benchmark problems were held in 2019 and 2020[1]. In the 2019 competition, the total mean PR values are 0.8916219 by HillVallEA19, 0.8851358 by HillVallEA, 0.8544251 by ANBNWI-DE, and so on. In the 2020 competition, the total mean PR values are 0.9063179 by RS-CMSA-ESII, 0.89225 by GaMeDE, 0.8334679 by CMSA-ES-DIPS, and so on. This study ranked third in both competitions, which is considered a satisfactory achievement.

7. Conclusions

We have proposed PSO with graph-based speciation (SPSO-G), a proximity graph β-relaxed RNG (βRNG), the dynamic control of β, the mutation and the crossover with adaptive control of the crossover rate to solve multimodal problems. In this study, we proposed two mutation

---

[1] https://github.com/mikeagn/CEC2013

Table 2. Experimental results of problems 1–10

	Function	ϵ	NMMSO	Imp.SPSO-G/βRNG	NoSM	NoLM	NoPar
1	F_1 (1D)	1.0e-01	1	1	1	1	1
		1.0e-02	1	1	1	1	1
		1.0e-03	1	1	1	1	1
		1.0e-04	1	1	1	1	1
		1.0e-05	1	1	1	1	1
		mean	1	1	1	1	1
2	F_2 (1D)	1.0e-01	1	1	1	1	1
		1.0e-02	1	1	1	1	1
		1.0e-03	1	1	1	1	1
		1.0e-04	1	1	1	1	1
		1.0e-05	1	1	1	1	1
		mean	1	1	1	1	1
3	F_3 (1D)	1.0e-01	1	1	1	1	1
		1.0e-02	1	1	1	1	1
		1.0e-03	1	1	1	1	1
		1.0e-04	1	1	1	1	1
		1.0e-05	1	1	1	1	1
		mean	1	1	1	1	1
4	F_4 (2D)	1.0e-01	1	1	1	1	1
		1.0e-02	1	1	1	1	1
		1.0e-03	1	1	1	1	1
		1.0e-04	1	1	1	1	1
		1.0e-05	1	1	1	1	1
		mean	1	1	1	1	1
5	F_5 (2D)	1.0e-01	1	1	1	1	1
		1.0e-02	1	1	1	1	1
		1.0e-03	1	1	1	1	1
		1.0e-04	1	1	1	1	1
		1.0e-05	1	1	1	1	1
		mean	1	1	1	1	1
6	F_6 (2D)	1.0e-01	0.998	1	1	1	1
		1.0e-02	0.994	1	1	1	1
		1.0e-03	0.992	1	1	1	1
		1.0e-04	0.992	1	1	1	1
		1.0e-05	0	1	1	1	1
		mean	0.7952	**1**	**1**	**1**	**1**
7	F_7 (2D)	1.0e-01	1	1	1	1	1
		1.0e-02	1	0.996667	0.983333	0.997778	0.996111
		1.0e-03	1	0.988889	0.957222	0.991111	0.988889
		1.0e-04	1	0.983333	0.93	0.988889	0.978889
		1.0e-05	1	0.977778	0.911667	0.987778	0.973333
		mean	**1**	0.989333	0.956444	0.993111	0.987444
8	F_6 (3D)	1.0e-01	0.954	0.979506	0.991358	0.99679	0.983457
		1.0e-02	0.939	0.971358	0.987407	0.994815	0.976296
		1.0e-03	0.922	0.96642	0.982222	0.991605	0.967901
		1.0e-04	0.899	0.958272	0.974568	0.987407	0.958765
		1.0e-05	0.87	0.947407	0.958765	0.982469	0.949136
		mean	0.9168	0.964593	0.978864	**0.990617**	0.967111
9	F_7 (3D)	1.0e-01	0.978	1	1	1	1
		1.0e-02	0.978	0.994722	0.894722	0.995926	0.995648
		1.0e-03	0.978	0.988611	0.813796	0.990926	0.990463
		1.0e-04	0.978	0.978796	0.747222	0.984537	0.986111
		1.0e-05	0.978	0.975278	0.704167	0.982593	0.983056
		mean	0.978	0.987481	0.831981	0.990796	**0.991056**
10	F_8 (2D)	1.0e-01	1	1	0.993333	1	1
		1.0e-02	1	1	0.993333	1	1
		1.0e-03	1	1	0.993333	1	1
		1.0e-04	1	1	0.993333	0.998333	0.998333
		1.0e-05	1	1	0.99	0.998333	0.995
		mean	**1**	**1**	0.992666	0.999333	0.998667

Table 3. Experimental results of problems 11–20

	Function	ϵ	NMMSO	Imp.SPSO-G/βRNG	NoSM	NoLM	NoPar
11	F_9 (2D)	1.0e-01	0.99	1	1	1	1
		1.0e-02	0.99	1	1	0.993333	1
		1.0e-03	0.99	1	1	0.963333	1
		1.0e-04	0.99	1	0.996667	0.96	1
		1.0e-05	0.99	1	0.993333	0.956667	1
		mean	0.99	**1**	0.998	0.974667	**1**
12	F_{10} (2D)	1.0e-01	0.995	0.9675	0.99	1	0.96
		1.0e-02	0.995	0.9675	0.9875	0.9975	0.9575
		1.0e-03	0.995	0.9675	0.9875	0.99	0.955
		1.0e-04	0.993	0.9675	0.9875	0.9825	0.955
		1.0e-05	0.99	0.9675	0.9875	0.9825	0.955
		mean	**0.9936**	0.9675	0.988	0.9905	0.9565
13	F_{11} (2D)	1.0e-01	0.99	0.896667	0.87	0.88	0.893333
		1.0e-02	0.987	0.883333	0.836667	0.846667	0.88
		1.0e-03	0.983	0.873333	0.783333	0.83	0.876667
		1.0e-04	0.983	0.87	0.776667	0.83	0.87
		1.0e-05	0.983	0.86	0.766667	0.826667	0.86
		mean	**0.9852**	0.876667	0.806667	0.842667	0.876
14	F_{11} (3D)	1.0e-01	0.77	0.763333	0.72	0.746667	0.76
		1.0e-02	0.74	0.756667	0.703333	0.72	0.74
		1.0e-03	0.723	0.743333	0.683333	0.696667	0.733333
		1.0e-04	0.72	0.74	0.68	0.696667	0.73
		1.0e-05	0.72	0.74	0.673333	0.696667	0.72
		mean	0.7346	**0.748667**	0.692	0.711334	0.736667
15	F_{12} (3D)	1.0e-01	0.65	0.745	0.7425	0.72	0.75
		1.0e-02	0.647	0.745	0.7425	0.72	0.75
		1.0e-03	0.642	0.745	0.74	0.72	0.75
		1.0e-04	0.632	0.745	0.74	0.72	0.75
		1.0e-05	0.632	0.745	0.74	0.72	0.75
		mean	0.6406	0.745	0.741	0.72	**0.75**
16	F_{11} (5D)	1.0e-01	0.66	0.673333	0.666667	0.666667	0.67
		1.0e-02	0.66	0.67	0.666667	0.666667	0.666667
		1.0e-03	0.66	0.666667	0.666667	0.666667	0.666667
		1.0e-04	0.66	0.666667	0.666667	0.666667	0.666667
		1.0e-05	0.66	0.666667	0.666667	0.666667	0.666667
		mean	0.66	**0.668667**	0.666667	0.666667	0.667334
17	F_{12} (5D)	1.0e-01	0.48	0.6575	0.6375	0.6175	0.635
		1.0e-02	0.477	0.6575	0.635	0.615	0.6325
		1.0e-03	0.47	0.655	0.625	0.615	0.6325
		1.0e-04	0.468	0.655	0.6175	0.615	0.6325
		1.0e-05	0.46	0.6525	0.6075	0.615	0.6325
		mean	0.471	**0.6555**	0.6245	0.6155	0.633
18	F_{11} (10D)	1.0e-01	0.65	0.66	0.663333	0.666667	0.666667
		1.0e-02	0.65	0.66	0.66	0.666667	0.666667
		1.0e-03	0.65	0.66	0.66	0.666667	0.666667
		1.0e-04	0.65	0.66	0.66	0.666667	0.666667
		1.0e-05	0.65	0.66	0.66	0.666667	0.666667
		mean	0.65	0.66	0.660667	**0.666667**	0.666667
19	F_{12} (10D)	1.0e-01	0.46	0.505	0.4975	0.5075	0.505
		1.0e-02	0.46	0.505	0.495	0.5075	0.505
		1.0e-03	0.457	0.505	0.49	0.5075	0.505
		1.0e-04	0.45	0.505	0.49	0.5075	0.505
		1.0e-05	0.437	0.505	0.49	0.5075	0.505
		mean	0.4528	0.505	0.4925	**0.5075**	0.505
20	F_{12} (20D)	1.0e-01	0.18	0.3825	0.3275	0.38	0.34
		1.0e-02	0.175	0.3725	0.3175	0.37	0.33
		1.0e-03	0.172	0.3575	0.3075	0.36	0.3075
		1.0e-04	0.172	0.3425	0.2875	0.345	0.29
		1.0e-05	0.172	0.3225	0.2775	0.275	0.2875
		mean	0.1742	**0.3555**	0.3035	0.346	0.311
	total mean PR		0.8221	**0.856195**	0.836673	0.850768	0.852322

operations and the parameter adjustment to enhance the local search ability.

We performed numerical experiments using benchmark problems for "CEC'2013 special session and competition on niching methods for multimodal function optimization". As for the total PR values, improved SPSO-G/βRNG attained the best result followed by improved SPSO-G/βRNG without parameter adjustment, improved SPSO-G/βRNG without the local mutation, without the sphere mutation, and NMMSO.

In problems 1–12, the proposed method can find more than 95% of optimal solutions. Also, the proposed method can find more than about 3/4 of optimal solutions in problems 13–15, and more than about 2/3 of optimal solutions in problems 16–18. However, the PR values in problem 19 and 20 are about 1/2 and 1/3, respectively. That is, PR values in functions with a large number of dimensions are extremely low. We will further investigate methods for efficiently dividing and searching multidimensional space. Also, we will apply the proposed graph and method to other population-based algorithms.

References

[1] Kennedy, J. and Eberhart, R. C., *Swarm Intelligence*, San Francisco: Morgan Kaufmann (2001).

[2] Sareni, B. and Krahenbuhl, L., "Fitness sharing and niching methods revisited", *IEEE Transactions on Evolutionary Computation*, Vol. 2, No. 3, pp. 97–106 (1998).

[3] Li, J.-P., Li, X. and Wood, A., "Species based evolutionary algorithms for multimodal optimization: A brief review", *IEEE Congress on Evolutionary Computation*, IEEE (2010), pp. 1–8.

[4] Li, X., "Efficient differential evolution using speciation for multimodal function optimization", *Proceedings of the 7th annual conference on Genetic and evolutionary computation* (2005), pp. 873–880.

[5] Shibasaka, M., Hara, A., Ichimura, T. and Takahama, T., "Species-based Differential Evolution with Switching Search Strategies for Multimodal Function Optimization", *Proc. of the 2007 IEEE Congress on Evolutionary Computation* (2007), pp. 1183–1190.

[6] Gao, W., Yen, G. G. and Liu, S., "A cluster-based differential evolution with self-adaptive strategy for multimodal optimization", *IEEE transactions on cybernetics*, Vol. 44, No. 8, pp. 1314–1327 (2014).

[7] Takahama, T. and Sakai, S., "Differential Evolution with Graph-Based Speciation by Competitive Hebbian Rules", *Proc. of the Sixth International Conference on Genetic and Evolutionary Computing (ICGEC2012)* (2012), pp. 445–448.

[8] Sakai, S. and Takahama, T., "A Comparative Study on Graph-Based Speciation Methods

for Species-Based Differential Evolution", M.Kitahara and C.Czerkawski (eds.), *Social Systems Solutions through Economic Sciences*, Fukuoka: Kyushu University Press, pp. 105–125 (2013).

[9] Takahama, T. and Sakai, S., "Multimodal optimization by particle swarm optimization with graph-based speciation using β-relaxed relative neighborhood graph and seed-centered mutation", *Artificial Life and Robotics*, Vol. 27, No. 2, pp. 236–247 (2022).

[10] Sakai, S. and Takahama, T., "A Study on Crossover Operations Using Hill-Valley Detection for Multimodal Optimization by Particle Swarm Optimization with Graph-Based Speciation", K.Ota, A.Nushimoto and T.Sakaguchi (eds.), *The Application of Economic Sciences to Civic Life and Local Economies*, Kyushu University Press, pp. 73–93 (2024).

[11] Li, X., Engelbrecht, A. and Epitropakis, M. G., "Benchmark functions for CEC'2013 special session and competition on niching methods for multimodal function optimization", *RMIT University, Evolutionary Computation and Machine Learning Group, Australia, Tech. Rep* (2013).

[12] Gabriel, K. R. and Sokal, R. R., "A New Statistical Approach to Geographic Variation Analysis", *Systematic Zoology*, Vol. 18, pp. 259–270 (1969).

[13] Toussaint, G. T., "The Relative Neighborhood Graph of a Finite Planar Set", *Pattern Recognition*, Vol. 12, No. 4, pp. 261–268 (1980).

[14] Kirkpatrick, D. G. and Radke, J. D., "A Framework for Computational Morphology", Toussaint, G. (ed.), *Computational Geometry*, North-Holland, pp. 217–248 (1985).

[15] Li, J.-P., Li, X.-D. and Wood, A., "Species Based Evolutionary Algorithms for Multimodal Optimization: A Brief Review", *Proc. of the 2010 IEEE Congress on Evolutionary Computation* (2010), pp. 1–8.

[16] Li, X., "Efficient Differential Evolution Using Speciation for Multimodal Function Optimization", *Proc. of the 2005 Conference on Genetic and Evolutionary Computation* (2005), pp. 873–880.

[17] Qu, B. and Suganthan, P., "Modified Species-Based Differential Evolution with Self-Adaptive Radius for Multi-Modal Optimization", *Proc. of the 2010 International Conference on Computational Problem-Solving* (2010), pp. 326–331.

[18] Kennedy, J. and Eberhart, R. C., "Particle Swarm Optimization", *Proc. of IEEE International Conference on Neural Networks*, Perth, Australia (1995), pp. 1942–1948.

[19] Eberhart, R. and Shi, Y., "Particle swarm optimization: developments, applications and resources", *Proc. of the 2001 Congress on Evolutionary Computation* (2001), pp. 81–86.

[20] Engelbrecht, A., "Particle swarm optimization: Global best or local best?", *2013 BRICS Congress on Computational Intelligence & 11th Brazilian Congress on Computational Intelligence*, IEEE (2013), pp. 124–135.

[21] Shi, Y. and Eberhart, R., "Empirical study of particle swarm optimization", *Proc. of the 1999 Congress on Evolutionary Computation* (1999), pp. 1945–1950.

[22] Bansal, J. C., Singh, P., Saraswat, M., Verma, A., Jadon, S. S. and Abraham, A., "Inertia weight strategies in particle swarm optimization", *Third world congress on nature and biologically inspired computing* (2011), pp. 640–647.

[23] Takahama, T. and Sakai, S., "Fuzzy C-Means Clustering and Partition Entropy for Species-Best Strategy and Search Mode Selection in Nonlinear Optimization by Differential Evolution", *Proc. of the 2011 IEEE International Conference on Fuzzy Systems* (2011), pp. 290–297.

[24] Fieldsend, J. E., "Running Up Those Hills: Multi-modal search with the niching migratory multi-swarm optimiser", *2014 IEEE Congress on Evolutionary Computation* (2014), pp. 2593–2600.

Contributors

Masayuki HIROMOTO, *Professor, Hiroshima Shudo University*

Masayuki HIROMOTO obtained an LL.M. at Osaka City University and an M.A. in Political Science at the University of New Orleans. His career as an academic started when he accepted the post of lecturer at the Faculty of Law, Hiroshima Shudo University, in 1999. His research covers policy networks and large city governments and aims to identify methodologies for effectively implementing policies or programs, receiving collaboration from various people to solve social problems, and activating communities with limited sources.

Hiroki IWATA, *Professor, Hiroshima Shudo University*

Hiroki IWATA obtained his Ph.D. in Economics from the Graduate School of Economics at Kyoto University in 2007. After working as a research fellow at Kyoto University and an assistant professor at Fukuoka Institute of Technology, he became an associate professor at the Faculty of Human Environmental Studies at Hiroshima Shudo University in 2013. In 2015, he was promoted to professor in the same department, a position he holds to this day. His specialization is in environmental economics, with his main research focusing on the impact of firms' environmental performance on economic performance, the relationship between global warming and economic activity, theoretical analysis of the emergence of green innovation, and the economic analysis of voluntary approaches such as eco-labeling.

Shohei KATAYAMA, *Professor, Hiroshima Shudo University*

Shohei KATAYAMA is a professor at the Faculty and Graduate School of Economic Sciences of Hiroshima Shudo University. He received the Master Degree of Economics and the Doctor Degree of Economics from Kobe University. He teaches courses in macroeconomics in the Faculty of Economic Sciences and macroeconomic policy in the Graduate School of Economic Sciences. His main research themes are the R&D-based growth, the secular stagnation in Japan and the decreasing population in Japan. He stayed at Brown University (1991-1992) and Stanford University (1996-1997), (2009-2010) as a visiting scholar.

Hiroyuki DEKIHARA, *Professor, Hiroshima Shudo University*

Hiroyuki DEKIHARA is a professor at the Faculty of Economic Sciences in Hiroshima Shudo University. He received his Ph.D. in Information Engineering from Hiroshima City University,

Japan, in 2003. From 2001 to 2016, he worked at Hiroshima International University, eventually as an associate professor. He joined Hiroshima Shudo University as an associate professor in 2017, and has been a professor since 2019. His research interests span C/S systems, data engineering, and information technology education. Much of his work has been on improving and developing mechanism of server that manages clients. He presented at a paper titled "An Extended Technique for R-tree to Manage Multiple Type Objects", Journal of Computational Methods in Sciences and Engineering, Vol.12, pp. S53-S61(2012). Currently, he is a member of research project developing educational frameworks and contents on key technologies of Forth Industrial Revolution: AI, IoT, Virtualization, etc.

Toru OCHI, *Assistant Professor*, *Osaka Institute of Technology*

Toru OCHI received his Master's degree in Informatics from Osaka Institute of Technology in 2002. He joined Hiroshima International University as an Assistant Professor in 2002. He gave lectures on Information Technology and Computer Network at the University. He joined Osaka Institute of Technology as an Associate Professor in 2013. He gives lectures on Information Technology and Unix at the University. His research interests are Information Technology Education, IoT and Artificial Intelligence. He has been a member of Information Processing Society of Japan (IPSJ), was the secretary of Special Interest Groups on Computer and Education from 2018 to 2021, and is a member of Editorial Committee of IPSJ Journal from 2021.

Minori KURAHASI, *Lecturer*, *Hagoromo University of International Studies*

Minori KURAHASI is a lecturer in Faculty of Social Sciences at Hagoromo University of International Studies. He received his Master's degree in literature from Kyoto University in 2003. He gave lectures on linguistics and phonetics in several universities as a part-time lecturer from 2004 to 2015. He was an associate professor in Cybermedia Center at Osaka University from 2015 to 2020. His research interests include research on information technology education and linguistics.

Masafumi IMAI, *Professor*, *Toyohashi Sozo University*

Masafumi IMAI is a Professor in Faculty of Business Administration at Toyohashi Sozo University. He received his Doctor of engineering from Tokyo Metropolitan University in 1997. His specialties are management system engineering, chaotic time series data prediction, etc. He is executive director and chairman of the public relations committee of the Japan Association for Management Systems.

Keiji TAGAMI, *Associate Professor*, *Hiroshima Shudo University*

Keiji TAGAMI recieved his Doctor of Science from Tokyo Institute of Technology in 2015. He was an assistant professor (without tenure) in Tokyo University of Science from 2016 to 2019, and an assistant professor in National Fisheries University from 2019 to 2022. In 2022, He joined Hiroshima Shudo University as an associate professor in Faculty of Economics Sciences. His research interests are Low-dimensional Topology and Knot Theory, with additional studies involving networks via topological techniques. Several of his works were supported by Japan Society for the Promotion of Science (JSPS) KAKENHI (Grant numbers 13J01362, 15J01087, 16H07230, 18K13416 and 22K13923). He has published papers in such journals as "Bulletin of the Belgian Mathematical Society - Simon Stevin", "Journal of the Korean Mathematical Society", "Canadian Journal of Mathematics", "Mathematical Research Letters", "International Journal of Mathematics", "Algebraic and Geometric Topology", "Hiroshima Mathematical Journal", "Tohoku Mathematical Journal" etc.

Setsuko SAKAI, *Professor*, *Hiroshima Shudo University*

Setsuko SAKAI graduated from the Faculty of Education, Fukui University, 1979. She finished her doctoral course of Informatics and Mathematical Science at Osaka University in 1984. She became a lecturer at the College of Business Administration and Information Science, Koshien University, in 1986, and then an associate professor of the Faculty of Education, Fukui University, in 1990. Since 1998, she has been with the Faculty of Commercial Sciences of Hiroshima Shudo University, where she is a professor in the Department of Business Administration. She is currently working on game theory, decision making, nonlinear optimization by direct search methods, evolutionary computation, swarm intelligence and fuzzy mathematical programming. She is a member of the Operations Research Society of Japan, Japan Society for Fuzzy Theory and Intelligent Informatics, the Japan Society for Production Management and IEEE. She holds a D. Eng. degree. She has published papers such as "Tuning fuzzy control rules by α constrained method which solves constrained nonlinear optimization problems"(1999) and "Reducing the Number of Function Evaluations in Differential Evolution by Estimated Comparison Method using an Approximation Model with Low Accuracy"(2008) in The Transactions of the Institute of Electronics, Information and Communication Engineers, "Fast and Stable Constrained Optimization by the ε Constrained Differential Evolution", in Pacific Journal of Optimization (2009), "Constrained Optimization by Improved Particle Swarm Optimization with the Equivalent Penalty Coefficient Method", in Artificial Life and Robotics (2020) and so on. She has also published papers in such journals as IEEE Transactions on Evolutionary Computation, Journal of Optimization Theory and its Applications, Transactions of the Japanese Society for Artificial Intelligence etc.

Tetsuyuki TAKAHAMA, *Professor, Hiroshima City University*

Tetsuyuki TAKAHAMA graduated from the Department of Electrical Engineering Ⅱ, Kyoto University, in 1982. He finished his doctoral course in 1987. He became an assistant professor, and then a lecturer, at Fukui University in 1994. Since 1998, he has been with the Graduate School of Information Sciences of Hiroshima City University, where he is a professor in the Department of Intelligent Systems. He is currently working on natural computing including evolutionary computation and swarm intelligence, nonlinear optimization and machine learning. He is a member of the Information Processing Society of Japan, the Japan Society for Artificial Intelligence, the Japanese Society of Information and Systems in Education, the Association for Natural Language Processing and IEEE. He holds a D. Eng. degree. He has published papers such as "Structural Optimization by Genetic Algorithm with Degeneration(GAd)", in The Transactions of the Institute of Electronics, Information and Communication Engineers (2003), "Constrained Optimization by Applying the α Constrained Methods to the Nonlinear Simplex Method with Mutations", in IEEE Transactions on Evolutionary Computation (2005), "Efficient Constrained Optimization by the ε Constrained Differential Evolution using an Approximation Model with Low Accuracy", in Transactions of the Japanese Society for Artificial Intelligence(2009), "Improving an Adaptive Differential Evolution Using Hill-Valley Detection" in International Journal of Hybrid Intelligent Systems (2016) and so on. He has also published papers in such journals as Information Processing Society of Japan Journal, International Journal of Innovative Computing, Information and Control Journal of Japan Society for Fuzzy Theory and Systems etc.

Series of Monographs of Contemporary Social Systems Solutions
Produced by
the Faculty of Economic Sciences, Hiroshima Shudo University

190 × 265 mm   5,000 yen (tax not included)

Volume 1   **Social Systems Solutions by Legal Informatics,**
           Economic Sciences and Computer Sciences
Edited by Munenori Kitahara and Kazunori Morioka   160 pages   ISBN 978-4-7985-0011-9

Volume 2   **The New Viewpoints and New Solutions of**
           Economic Sciences in the Information Society
Edited by Shusaku Hiraki and Nan Zhang   160 pages   ISBN 978-4-7985-0055-3

Volume 3   **Social Systems Solutions Applied by Economic Sciences**
           and Mathematical Solutions
Edited by Minenori Kitahara and Chris Czerkawski   156 pages   ISBN 978-4-7985-0078-2

Volume 4   **Social Systems Solutions through Economic Sciences**
Edited by Munenori Kitahara and Chris Czerkawski   156 pages   ISBN 978-4-7985-0097-3

Volume 5   **Legal Informatics, Economic Science and Mathematical**
           Research
Edited by Munenori Kitahara and Chris Czerkawski   104 pages   ISBN 978-4-7985-0125-3

Volume 6   **New Solutions in Legal Informatics, Economic Sciences**
           and Mathematics
Edited by Munenori Kitahara and Kazuaki Okamura   160 pages   ISBN 978-4-7985-0152-9

Volume 7   **Contemporary Works in Economic Sciences:**
           Legal Informatics, Economics, OR and Mathematics
Edited by Munenori Kitahara and Hiroaki Teramoto   130 pages   ISBN 978-4-7985-0179-6

Volume 8   **Challenging Researches in Economic Sciences:**
           Legal Informatics, Environmental Economics, Economics,
           OR and Mathematics
Edited by Munenori Kitahara and Hiroaki Teramoto   152 pages   ISBN 978-4-7985-0206-9

Volume 9   **Recent Studies in Economic Sciences:**
           Information Systems, Project Managements, Economics,
           OR and Mathematics
Edited by Atsushi Kadoya and Hiroaki Teramoto   126 pages   ISBN 978-4-7985-0229-8

Volume 10 **Advanced Studies in Economic Sciences: Information Systems, Economics and OR**
Edited by Kazunori Morioka and Atsushi Kadoya   104 pages ISBN 978-4-7985-0258-8

Volume 11 **Current Researches for Applied Economics, Information Systems, Mathematics and OR**
Edited by Atsushi Kadoya and Jun-ichi Maeda   116 pages ISBN 978-4-7985-0283-0

Volume 12 **New Approaches for Operations Research and Applied Economics**
Edited by Jun-ichi Maeda, Kazuaki Okamura and Hiroyuki Dekihara
96 pages ISBN 978-4-7985-0306-6

Volume 13 **Operations Research and Information Systems**
Edited by Jun-ichi Maeda, Kazuaki Okamura and Hiroyuki Dekihara
90 pages ISBN 978-4-7985-0326-4

Volume 14 **Economic History, Flow of Funds, Information Systems and Operations Research**
Edited by Koshiro Ota, Jun-ichi Maeda and Aya Nushimoto
110 pages ISBN 978-4-7985-0349-3

Volume 15 **The Application of Economic Sciences to Civic Life and Local Economies**
Edited by Koshiro Ota, Aya Nushimoto and Takuya Sakaguchi
114 pages ISBN978-4-7985-0371-4